For Sharon,
to inspire you!

Fredrille

IPPA 2013

Handbook of Solution-Focused Conflict Management

Acknowledgments

I will listen to you, especially when we disagree
Barack Obama (Acceptance Speech)

An author never writes a book alone. It is always a product of many people who work together and ultimately ensure that the name of the author appears on the cover.

I thank my husband, Hidde, and my daughters, Eva and Eline, for giving me the opportunity and encouragement to write my books. I thank my friends, colleagues, students and clients, my publisher, and translators Inge, Steve, and Paula, and everyone else who has contributed to the realization of this book. Grazie also to my Italian cats for keeping me company during the many pleasant hours of thinking and writing.

A special word of thanks goes to my inspiring colleague Ken Cloke for his willingness to write the Foreword and Epilogue.

Handbook of Solution-Focused Conflict Management

Fredrike Bannink

With a Foreword and Epilogue by Kenneth Cloke

HOGREFE

Library of Congress Cataloging in Publication

is available via the Library of Congress Marc Database under the
LC Control Number 2010904393

Library and Archives Canada Cataloguing in Publication

Bannink, Fredrike
    Handbook of solution-focused conflict management / Fredrike Bannink ; with a
foreword and epilogue by Kenneth Cloke.

Includes bibliographical references.
ISBN 978-0-88937-384-6

    1. Conflict management. 2. Interpersonal relations. I. Title.

HD42.B26 2010   658.4'053   C2010-902263-7

© 2010 by Hogrefe Publishing

PUBLISHING OFFICES
USA: Hogrefe Publishing, 875 Massachusetts Avenue, 7th Floor,
                Cambridge, MA 02139
                Phone (866) 823-4726, Fax (617) 354-6875;
                E-mail customerservice@hogrefe-publishing.com
EUROPE: Hogrefe Publishing, Rohnsweg 25, 37085 Göttingen, Germany
                Phone +49 551 49609-0, Fax +49 551 49609-88,
                E-mail publishing@hogrefe.com

SALES & DISTRIBUTION
USA: Hogrefe Publishing, Customer Services Department,
                30 Amberwood Parkway, Ashland, OH 44805
                Phone (800) 228-3749, Fax (419) 281-6883,
                E-mail customerservice@hogrefe.com
EUROPE: Hogrefe Publishing, Rohnsweg 25, 37085 Göttingen, Germany
                Phone +49 551 49609-0, Fax +49 551 49609-88,
                E-mail publishing@hogrefe.com

OTHER OFFICES
CANADA: Hogrefe Publishing, 660 Eglinton Ave. East, Suite 119-514, Toronto,
                Ontario, M4G 2K2
SWITZERLAND: Hogrefe Publishing, Länggass-Strasse 76, CH-3000 Bern 9

Hogrefe Publishing
Incorporated and registered in the Commonwealth of Massachusetts, USA, and in Göttingen,
Lower Saxony, Germany

Printed and bound in the USA
ISBN: 978-0-88937-384-6

Foreword: Building Bridges Between Psychology and Conflict Resolution — Implications for Mediator Learning

Over the last three decades, hundreds of thousands of people around the world have been trained in community, divorce, family, commercial, organizational, and workplace mediation, as well as in allied conflict resolution skills such as collaborative negotiation, group facilitation, public dialogue, restorative justice, victim-offender mediation, ombudsmanship, collaborative law, consensus decision making, creative problem solving, prejudice reduction and bias awareness, conflict resolution systems design, and dozens of associated practices.

Among the most important and powerful of these skills are a number of core ideas and interventions that originate in psychology, particularly in what is commonly known as "brief therapy," where the border separating conflict resolution from psychological intervention has become indistinct, and in many places blurred beyond recognition. Examples of the positive consequences of blurring this line can be found in recent discoveries in neurophysiology, "emotional intelligence," and solution-focused approaches to conflict resolution.

While it is, of course, both necessary and vital that we recognize the key differences between the professions of psychology and conflict resolution, it is more necessary and vital, especially in these times, that we recognize their essential similarities, collaborate in developing creative new techniques, and invite them to learn as much as they can from each other.

Beyond this, I believe it is increasingly important for us to consciously generate a fertile, collaborative space between them; discourage the tendency to jealously guard protected territory; and oppose efforts to create new forms of private property in techniques that reduce hostility and relieve suffering.

It is therefore critical that we think carefully and strategically about how best to translate a deeper understanding of the emotional and neurophysiological underpinnings of conflict and resolution processes into practical, hands-on mediation techniques; that we explore the evolving relationship between mediation and psychology, and other professions as well; and that we translate that understanding into improved ways of helping people become competent, successful mediators, as Fredrike Bannink sets out to do in the present volume.

Among the urgent reasons for doing so are the rise of increasingly destructive global conflicts that cannot be solved even by a single nation, let alone by a single style, approach, profession, or technique; the persistence of intractable conflicts that require more advanced techniques; and the recent rise of innovative, transformational techniques that form only a small part of the curriculum of most mediation trainings. The present generation is being asked a profound set of questions that require immediate action based on complex, diverse, complementary, even contradictory answers. In my judgment, these questions include:

- What is our responsibility as global citizens for solving the environmental, social, economic, and political conflicts that are taking place around us?

- Is it possible to successfully apply conflict resolution principles to the inequalities, inequities, and dysfunctions that are continuing to fuel chronic social, economic, and political conflicts?
- Can we find ways of working beyond national, religious, ethnic, and professional borders so as to strengthen our capacity for international collaboration and help save the planet?
- Can we build bridges across diverse disciplines so as to integrate the unique understandings and skills that other professions have produced regarding conflict and resolution?
- How can we use this knowledge to improve the ways we impact mediator learning so as to better achieve these goals?

Locating potential synergies between psychology and conflict resolution will allow us to take a few small steps toward answering these questions. And small steps, as we learn in mediation, are precisely what are needed to achieve meaningful results. Why should we consider the possibilities of ego defenses or solution-focused mediation? For the same reasons we consider the potential utility of a variety of interventions – because they allow us to understand conflict and enter it in unique and useful ways.

The logical chain that connects conflict resolution with psychology is simple yet inexorable and logically rigorous, which proceeds as follows:

- It is possible for people to disagree with each other without experiencing conflict.
- What distinguishes conflict from disagreement is the presence of what are commonly referred to as "negative" emotions, such as anger, fear, guilt, and shame.
- Thus, every conflict, by definition, contains an indispensible emotional element.
- Conflicts can only be reached and resolved in their emotional location by people who have acquired emotional processing skills, or what Daniel Goleman broadly describes as "emotional intelligence."
- The discipline that is most familiar with these emotional dynamics is psychology.
- Therefore, mediation can learn from psychology how to be more effective in resolving conflicts.

It is my hope that this book by Fredrike Bannink will begin to change our ideas about the usefulness of psychological approaches in mediation. Hopefully, these ideas, exercises, and practices will encourage us to look more deeply and wisely at the world within, as well as the world without, and assist us in finding ways to translate our own suffering into methods and understandings that will lead to a better, less hostile and adversarial world.

Kenneth Cloke
Center for Dispute Resolution, Santa Monica, California, USA
President, Mediators Beyond Borders

Peer Commentaries

"Nearly everyone thinks of conflict resolution as focused on solutions, but exactly *how* this is to be done has remained something of a mystery – until now. Fredrike Bannink offers dozens of ideas, strategies, and techniques that can be used by conflict resolution practitioners to improve their effectiveness. A very useful book."

Kenneth Cloke, Mediator and President, Mediators Beyond Borders, USA

"As usual Fredrike Bannink writes with clarity and knowledge. This book draws together proof from many sources to support her central teachings. The results of these discoveries will help you to use her suggestions in new ways and in new settings."

Alasdair Macdonald, Psychiatrist and Trainer for Cooperation in the Workplace, UK

"With solution-focused conflict management a unique approach to mediation is presented that in the coming years will find its place along with other already existing models. What is special about it certainly becomes clear in this book."

Friedrich Glasl, Mediator, Austria

"I am very impressed how Fredrike Bannink develops the ideas, tools, and attitudes of solution-focused conflict management so clearly and comprehensively. Especially the step-by-step way she presents good solution-focused questions, describes their effects, and connects them with clear examples from many different areas of life makes it easy to follow. For those already acquainted with conflict resolution I see great potential for gathering new impulses and ideas that are easy to use and implement in their interventions."

Peter Roehrig, Coach and Mediator, Germany

"This book made me realize that a conflict is only a chance to exercise our own ability to bring peace and satisfaction to our own lives and to those of others. And it beautifully illustrates how we can experience the joy of developing ourselves into wiser human beings if we can cross the borders of difference with a positive shift in focus of attention. Many Japanese people might re-learn this spirit of harmony in our tradition with renewed wisdom".

Yasuteru Aoki, President, Solution Focus Consulting Inc., Japan

"Fredrike Bannink's *Handbook of Solution-Focused Conflict Management* is a valuable addition to the growing literature for mediation professionals, providing new and useful insights into the theory and application of the solution-focus approach to conflict management. Mediators, both new and experienced, will find this handbook an important resource for developing more effective techniques for assisting parties to resolve their disputes by achieving maximum non-zero cooperative outcomes while restoring relationships or ending them in a less hostile and confrontational manner. Coming from her experience as a clinical psychologist, Bannink cogently demonstrates why mediators should encourage participants to focus their attention on finding solutions rather than dwelling on the historical facts behind the problems as the preferred path to conflict resolution."

Myer J. Sankary, Mediator-Lawyer, ADR Services, Inc., Los Angeles; Past President of the Southern California Mediation Association, USA

"Fredrike Bannink's *Handbook of Solution-Focused Conflict Management* offers an important guide to bending conflict situations toward improved ends. Few people enjoy dealing with conflict, but the options, leaving things unattended or pursuing litigation, are almost always worse. Bannink moves us beyond traditional approaches to solution-focused models that assist participants to be at their best. Solution-focused conflict management insists that participants maintain responsibility for finding their own best solutions. Bannink's book moves us beyond barely sufficient dialogue and barely sufficient solutions to most capable dialogue and most capable solutions."

James C. Melamed, JD, CEO of Mediate.com, USA

Table of Contents

1 Bloodtaking and Peacemaking

Be the change you want to see in the world
Mahatma Gandhi

Conflict Management Is of All Times and All Species

More people are said to have died in wars during the twentieth century than in all earlier centuries combined. Every day the newspapers carry stories of people killing other people for money, to avenge a perceived wrong, or for no apparent reason at all. Among all the questions that can be asked about human social relations, none are more fraught with concern and uncertainty than questions about the causes of aggression and the means of controlling it.

Aggression and competition are the natural state of affairs in both human society and the animal kingdom. Our species relies heavily on cooperation for survival, as do many others, from wolves to dolphins to monkeys. Reconciliation and compromise are therefore as much a part of our heritage as is waging war. Chimpanzees kiss mouth-to-mouth and embrace after a fight. They use appeasement and reassurance gestures, like grooming, grunting, and holding hands. Spotted hyenas, thought to be a particularly aggressive species, are known to use reconciliation to restore damaged relationships. There are sound evolutionary reasons for these peacemaking tendencies. The human race would have long since been extinct if we did not reconcile. Therefore, conflict management is of all times and many, if not all, species.

One of the oldest examples of conflict management can be found in the Bible. In the passage Kings 3:16–28, two mothers approach King Solomon, bringing with them a baby boy. Each mother presents the same story. She and the other woman live together. One night, soon after the birth of their respective children, the other woman woke to find that she had smothered her own baby in her sleep. In anguish and jealousy, she took her dead son and exchanged it with the other's child. The following morning, the woman discovered the dead baby, and soon realized that it was not her own son, but the other woman's.

After some deliberation, Solomon calls for a sword. He declares that there is only one fair solution: The live son must be split in two, each woman receiving half of the child. Upon hearing this terrible verdict, the boy's true mother cries out, "Please, My Lord, give her the live child, do not kill him!" The liar, in her bitter jealousy, exclaims, "It shall be neither mine nor yours – divide it!" Solomon gives the baby to the real mother, realizing that the true mother's instincts were to protect her child, while the liar revealed that she did not truly love the child.

In the Middle Ages there were no formal systems of justice with which to control society. Men and woman handled conflict situations though through a wide variety of social and cultural values and rules. There was bloodtaking and peacemaking; there was retaliation and reconciliation. There were wars and crusades and there were gifts and rituals to end them.

People living in Somalia (East Africa) told me a striking example of the difficult choice they face between retaliation and reconciliation, which has been going on for many centuries. When a member of their clan is killed, the clan members have two choices: They may ask for 100 (depending on the status of the person murdered) camels from the clan of the murderer and there can be peace (reconciliation), or they may kill a member of the other clan with the same status as the person who was killed (retaliation). Since one camel costs around 500 US dollars and not many clans can afford or are willing to pay 50,000 US dollars, the obvious choice is retaliation. The answer to that killing is, of course, another killing, and so on, and so on. To this day in other parts in Africa, it is the family who decides what will happen to the murderer of one of their members. The murderer is thrown into the river and then the family decides on the spot whether they will save him and let him live (reconciliation) or let him drown (retaliation).

Modern Conflict Management

The new millennium brings to light several social evolutions. These changes are visible in different fields. In mental health care, for example, there is the evolution from lengthy to shorter forms of treatment. Due to the growing emancipation of the client, the medical model in which the professional is the expert is increasingly being questioned. This cause-and-effect model in psychotherapy, where the professional first needs to explore and analyze the problem, is being replaced by a solution-focused model. The same shift from a model with its focus on problems and how to treat them to a solution-focused model is seen in education, in management and coaching, and in organizations.

An evolution is also taking place within the administration of justice: Rather than using a judge, who makes a decision for the clients, the evolutionary process leads to forms of alternative dispute resolution (ADR). Mediation, one of these forms, involves a mediator, who acts as a facilitator and neutral (or, rather, multipartial) third party to help clients solve their conflict. Using mediation instead of the courtroom, conflicts can often be resolved more rapidly (and at an earlier stage), more economically, and with a more satisfying outcome for the clients. Mediation can take place between persons, between persons and institutions or companies, between institutions or companies, between persons and the government, and between groups of people or countries.

Psychology has until recently been concerned with identifying human weakness and correcting or amerliorating it. Now, *positive psychology* arises – a psychology of hope, optimism, and resilience – that perhaps someday will illuminate what human life at its best can be and show how we can help people make their lives good lives. The same applies to conflict management that, until recently, has been concerned with exploration and analysis of the conflict before correcting or ameliorating it.

Let me introduce *solution-focused conflict management*, a form of *positive conflict management*. Solution building is different from problem solving, as will be demonstrated in this book. Solution-focused conflict management no longer focuses on the conflict itself, but on what clients want to change in their lives and how to make that happen. It is about their "best case scenario," or even their "good enough case scenario," instead of their "worst case scenario." Solution-focused conflict management – focusing on hope, optimism, self-efficacy, resilience, competencies, and possibilities – offers new ways to form or strengthen relationships encouraging trust and respect or, alternatively, to end relationships in as pleasant a manner as possible. Solution-focused conflict management, sometimes called *solution-focused mediation*, is applicable in all settings where there is a conflict and people decide to do something about it, from divorce conflicts, family and neighbor conflicts, team and labor conflicts, personal injury conflicts, to international conflicts. May this book help you to help your clients make their lives good, and even better, lives.

Story 1: Taking a Different View

A traveler was riding along on his camel when he encountered three brothers deep in argument. He stopped, dismounted and inquired why they were fighting. The eldest brother explained that, some months earlier, their father had died and bequeathed all his camels to his three sons. His will was clear and explicit. The eldest son was to receive one half of the camels. The second was to receive one third. The third was to inherit one ninth. They had no dispute about that. The problem, and reason for their conflict, arose from the fact that the father had left them seventeen camels.

Almost anyone could appreciate the brothers' dilemma. Seventeen is not divisible by those proportions. 'We have tried every mathematical approach we can think of' they explained to the traveler. 'We have even considered killing and dismembering one or more of the camels to ensure that each received his bequeathed proportion. However, our father's will was clear on that too: the camels were to be passed on as livestock and not killed.' Each brother agreed that there was no value in receiving the odd limb or two of a dead beast.

In their failure to find a solution, they became frustrated and fell into argument. Half of seventeen was eight and a half. They couldn't kill a beast to divide it, so the elder suggested he take nine. The younger two objected. His greed would deprive them of their rightful inheritance. He should take eight, according to them, but he was not willing to receive less than his father had willed him. The argument raged, tempers became frayed, and the brothers fought bitterly. Each wanted what he rightfully considered his. None was willing to compromise.

'I see your dilemma,' said the stranger. 'Your father has given you a difficult challenge. I also think I see a solution.' He led his own camel across to the corral that contained the seventeen camels. He pushed the slip-rail aside, let his own enter, then closed off the corral again. Eighteen camels stood in the enclosure.

'Now' he said to the elder, 'you take your portion of one half.' The brother counted out the nine camels that he delightedly claimed for himself. He thanked the stranger for getting him his rightful share. Turning to the second brother, the traveler said 'Now you take your portion of one third.' This brother happily took his six camels and let them aside. To the third brother the stranger said 'Now it is your turn. Take your one ninth.' With relief, the last brother took his two camels and tethered them to the railing. This, of course, left behind the saddled camel on which the stranger had arrived.

'Your father has bequeathed you more than his camels' said the traveler. 'He has also left you something of his wisdom. In setting you this challenge what else do you think that he has given you?'

'I think' said the first brother, 'that he was trying to teach us that every problem has a solution. No matter how impossible something might seem, we may solve it by seeking a different perspective.' The second brother added 'I think it is more than that. As brothers we are always fighting. Father was always our arbitrator. He wanted us to realize that to survive as a family without him we needed a constructive and cooperative relationship. He set us a challenge that meant we needed to work together to find the solution. When greed and selfishness separated us, no one was happy.'

'I believe' said the third, 'he was possibly teaching us even more. He was saying that no matter how much each of us thinks we are right, we may not have the answer. Sometimes we need to look outside of ourselves. Sometimes, somebody else can offer us a different perspective and thus enable us to find a solution.'

The stranger smiled as he mounted his camel and prepared to move on. 'Perhaps one of you is right' he said. 'Perhaps all three are correct. Then again, maybe he was teaching you something even more.........'

2 Background Issues

Failing to plan is planning to fail
Mihaly Csikszentmihalyi

Introduction

Let me introduce to you four theoretical issues that are connected with solution-focused conflict management. The first connection is with *game theory*, explaining how mediation can be seen as an example of a nonzero sum game, where both players may win. The connection with *quantum mechanics* and *neuroscience* shows how a positive focus can change the way we solve conflict. The connection with *hope theory* shows the importance of having a destination, a map, and a means of transport to reach the preferred outcome in conflict. The connection with the *broaden-and-build theory*, finally, shows how, in contrast to negative emotions that narrow our thought-action repertoires, positive emotions broaden our thought-action repertoires and build enduring personal resources physically, intellectually, psychologically, and socially.

Game Theory

Nobel Prize winners Von Neumann and Morgenstern invented game theory in 1944 (Von Neumann & Morgenstern, 1944). They made a basic distinction between *zero-sum games* and *nonzero-sum games*. In zero-sum games, the fortunes of the players are inversely related, one contestant's gain is the other's loss, as in tennis or chess. In nonzero-sum games, one player's gain need not be bad news for the other(s). In highly nonzero-sum games, the players' interests can overlap entirely. Wright (2000) gives the example of the three Apollo 13 astronauts who were trying to figure out how their stranded spaceship could be repaired to get back to earth. The outcome was good for all (or could have been bad for all).

Bill Clinton stated in an interview:

In game theory, a zero-sum game is one where, in order for on person to win, somebody has to lose. A non-zero sum game is a game in which you can win and the person you are playing with can win as well. The more complex societies get and the more complex the networks of inter-dependence within and beyond community and national borders get, the more people are forced in their own interest to find non-zero sum solutions, that is, win-win solutions instead of win-lose solutions (Breslau & Heron, 2000).

Nonzero sum games are also played in biological and cultural evolution: If you are in the same boat, you will tend to perish unless you are conducive to productive cooperation.

Zero-sum games are a special case of constant-sum games in which choices by players can neither increase nor decrease the available resources. In zero-sum games, the total benefit to all players, for every combination of strategies, always adds to zero. Poker exemplifies a zero-sum game, because one wins exactly the amount one's opponents lose.

Many games studied by game theorists are nonzero-sum games, because some outcomes have net results greater than (positive sum games) or less than zero (negative sum games). In nonzero-sum games, a gain by one player does not necessarily correspond with a loss by another. The best metaphor for a non-zero-sum game is "being in the same boat." You sink (negative sum) or float (positive sum) together.

The classic example of a nonzero-sum game is the *prisoner's dilemma.* In that scenario, two partners in crime are being interrogated separately. The state lacks the evidence to convict them of the crime they committed but does have enough evidence to convict both on a lesser charge, bringing one-year prison term for each. The prosecutor wants a conviction on the more serious charge, and pressures each man individually to confess and implicate the other, saying, "If you confess but your partner does not, I will let you off free and use your testimony to lock him up for ten years. And if you do not confess, yet your partner does, you go to prison for ten years. If you confess and your partner does too, I will put you both away, but only for three years." The question is: will the two prisoners cooperate with each other, both refusing to confess? Or will one or both of them betray the other?

The outcome is determined by the expectations that each player forms of how the other will play, where each of them knows that their expectations are substantially reciprocal. Nonzero-sum games are not about relationships in which cooperation is necessarily taking place. They usually involve a relationship in which, if cooperation did take place, it would benefit both parties. Whether the cooperation does take place – whether the parties realize positive sums – is another matter. Sometimes in nonzero-sum situations, the object of the game is not to reap positive sums, but simply to avoid negative sums.

To realize mutual profit in a nonzero-sum situation, two problems must be solved: communication and trust. There are two pitfalls in nonzero-sum games:

There is the problem of cheating, and there is also a zero-sum dimension in almost any real-life nonzero-sum game.

> When you buy a car, the transaction is nonzero sum: you and the dealer both profit, which is why you both agree to the deal. But there is more than one price at which you both profit: the whole range between the highest you would rationally pay and the lowest the dealer would rationally accept. And within that range, you and the dealer are playing a zero-sum game: your gain is the dealer's loss. That's the reason bargaining takes place at car dealerships. (Wright, 2000, p. 25).

Schelling (1960) states that conflicts are typically mixtures of cooperative and competitive processes. The course of the conflict is determined by the nature of this mixture. The core emphasis is on having interdependent interests: The fates of clients are woven together. Game theory recognizes that cooperative as well as competitive interest may be intertwined in conflict.

In addition to interdependence, there can be independence, such that the activities and fate of the people involved do not affect one another. If they are completely independent of one another, no conflict arises. The existence of a conflict implies some form of interdependence. In a relationship, asymmetry may exist to the degree of interdependence. One person can be more dependent on the other than the other way around. In an extreme case, one person may be completely independent of the other, whereas the other may be completely dependent on the first person. As a consequence, that person will have greater power and influence in the relationship than the other person has.

From the perspective of game theory, mediation revolves around a nonzero-sum game, where everybody gains (win-win), whereas a judicial procedure revolves around a zero-sum game (win-lose). Win-win means you swim together; win-lose means you swim and the other party sinks or the other party swims and you sink, and lose-lose means you sink together.

In mediation, the measure of success is not so much whether a client wins at the other client's expense, but whether he gets what he wants because he enables the other(s) to achieve their dreams and to do what they want. In other words: "Winning will depend on not wanting other people(s) to lose" (Wright, 2000, p. 332).

Quantum Mechanics and Neuroscience

Quantum mechanics is the study of the relationship between quanta and elementary particles. Its effects are typically not observable on a macroscopic scale, but become evident at atomic and subatomic levels. It introduced new physical principles and new dynamical laws.

One important finding of quantum mechanics is the so-called *uncertainty principle*, discovered by Nobel Prize winner Heisenberg. If we want to measure the position and momentum of a particular particle, we must see the particle and focus on it. This gives an uncertainty in the particle position. Quantum systems do seem to behave differently if we observe them. In other words, the subject who observes modifies the object that is observed. The human brain is also a quantum environment and is therefore subject to all the surprising laws of quantum mechanics. One of these laws is the quantum zeno effect (QZE). This effect is related to the observer effect of quantum physics. The behavior and position of any atom-sized entity, such as an atom, electron, or ion, appears to change when that entity is observed.

The QZE was linked with what happens when close attention is paid to a mental experience. Applied to neuroscience, the QZE states that the mental act of focusing attention stabilizes the associated brain circuits. So concentrating on any mental experience, whether a thought, a picture, or an emotion, maintains the brain state arising in association with that experience. Eventually this leads to physical changes in the brain's structure. Attention continually reshapes the patterns of the brain and the brain changes as a function of where an individual puts his attention: *The power is in the focus*. New brain circuits can be stabilized and thus developed (the neuroscientist's term for this is *self-directed neuroplasticity*). The neural net of the brain can activate a set of anatomically and chronologically associated firings in response to the environment. This profile is encoded, stored, and retrieved on the basis of a simple axiom defined by Hebb (1949): Neurons which fire together at one time will tend to fire together in the future. It is also possible for the brain to relocate brain activity associated with a certain function from one area to another, for instance, in a case of brain damage. And everyday thousands of new cells are created in the adult brain (neurogenesis), which was long thought to be impossible.

Seligman (2002), founder of the *positive psychology* movement (www.ted.com) found in a study with severely depressed individuals that positive behavior change is primarily a function of the ability to focus attention on specific – positive – ideas closely enough, often enough, and for a long enough time.

This is to say that it is wise to leave problem – or conflict – behaviors in the past and focus on identifying and creating new behaviors by first picturing these new behaviors in your mind and developing positive new mental maps that have the potential to become hardwired circuitry. This is best achieved through a solution-focused questioning approach that facilitates self-insight rather than through advice giving.

From the perspective of quantum mechanics, an objective world independent from personal perceptions is not real. Human conflicts are, per essence, subjective because they originate in the dynamics of personal thoughts, emotions, and beliefs of the people involved. The sources of personal conflicts are the result of the perceptions of persons. Einstein (1954) stated:

- Problems cannot be solved by the level of awareness that created them.
- We cannot solve problems by using the same kind of thinking we used when we created them.
- Significant problems cannot be solved at the same level of thinking we were at when we created them.
- No problem can be solved from the same consciousness that created it.

He postulated that information and knowledge is not sufficient for conflict resolution. Imagination is more important than knowledge, for knowledge is limited, whereas imagination embraces the entire world – stimulating progress and giving birth to evolution. As this book will show, imagination is widely used in the solution-focused approach using the *miracle question* and other hypothetical questions described in Chapters 5 and 6.

Recent insights in the field of neurobiology and knowledge about the functioning of both cerebral hemispheres (Siegel, 1999) show that the right hemisphere deals principally with processing nonverbal aspects of communication, such as seeing images and feeling primary emotions. The right hemisphere is involved in the understanding of metaphors, paradoxes, and humor. Reading fiction and poetry activates the right hemisphere, whereas the reading of scientific texts essentially activates the left hemisphere. There, the processes relating to the verbal meaning of words, also called "digital representations," take place. The left hemisphere is occupied with logical analyses (cause-effect relations). Linear processes occurring are reading the words in a sentence, aspects of attention, and discovering order in the events of a story. The left hemisphere thus dominates our language-based communication. Some authors are of the opinion that the right hemisphere sees the world more as it is and has a better overview of the context, whereas the left hemisphere tends to departmentalize the information received. The left hemisphere sees the trees, the right hemisphere the forest. Try listening to a favorite piece of music through headphones, first with your left ear, then with your right; what differences do you experience? Several studies have shown that most (right-handed) people prefer to listen to music with their left ear (connected to the right hemisphere), rather than with their right ear (connected to the left hemisphere). If one listens to music with the left ear, this gives a more holistic sensation, "a floating with the flow of the music," whereas the experience is different if one listens with the right ear. This tendency is reversed in professional musicians. An explanation for this is that they listen to music in a more analytical way than the casual listener. My supposition is that working in a solution-focused manner, thus with a high utilization of the imagination, such as "mental rehearsal" and hypothetical questions, particularly stimulates the nonverbal and holistic capacities of the right hemisphere. Not only the left hemisphere is engaged, as it is in (analytical) problem-focused working. The success of solution-focused conversations might be (partly) explained in the way it addresses both hemispheres of the brain.

Hope Theory

In Greek mythology, Pandora was the first woman, comparable to Eve. Zeus ordered Hephaestus to mould her out of Earth as part of the punishment of mankind for Prometheus' theft of the secret fire, and all the gods joined in offering

Pandora seductive gifts, one being curiosity. She was also given a jar and told that as long as she did not open the jar, nothing bad was ever going to happen. According to the myth, Pandora opened the jar, referred to in modern accounts as "Pandora's box," out of simple curiosity thereby releasing all the evils of mankind, all the plagues, and pestilence and evil that now exists in the world. Biting, stinging creatures flew through the air and attacked mortals; but the only one remaining behind in the box was hope, in those days considered the worst of all evils.

The phenomenon of hope has attracted the attention of many writers and philosophers. The Greek philosophers and the later Greek literature tended to the view that since fate was unchangeable, hope was an illusion: "I know how men in exile feed on dreams of hope," (Aeschylus, 525–456 BC) and "man's curse" (Euripides, 480–406 BC), because it only prolonged suffering.

Then, something changed. The Greek philosopher Aristotle (384–322 BC) had a more positive outlook on hope: "Hope is a waking dream." Aristotle mentions hope and hopefulness in several contexts, but most notably in his discussions of courage (Aristotle, 2004).

Cicero, a Roman politician (106–43 BC) stated, "While there's life, there's hope." Since the earliest of the Christian writers, hope has been considered one of the three major theological virtues: Faith, Love, and Hope. St. Paul wrote to Greek friends to declare that hope should stand along with love. Luther, like St. Paul, shook his fist at Greek fatalism and declared, "Everything that is done in the world is done by hope."

Since the 1950s, physicians and psychologists have pointed to the role of hope in health and well-being. In his 1959 address to the American Psychiatric Association, Menninger suggested that the power of hope was an untapped source of strength and healing for patients. He defined hope as "a positive expectancy of goal attainment" and "an adventure, a going forward, a confident search" (Menninger, 1959, p. 484). Menninger stated that hope was an indispensable factor in psychiatric treatment and psychiatric education.

In 1991, Snyder et al. proposed a two-factor cognitive model of hope that similarly focuses on goal attainment. Not only does Snyder focus on expectancies, but also on the motivation and planning that are necessary to attain goals. He defines hope as "a positive emotional state that is based on an interactively derived sense of successful (a) agency and (b) pathways (planning to meet goals)." Based on this definition, hope's agency or "willpower" component provides the determination to achieve goals, whereas its pathways or "waypower" component promotes the creation of alternative paths to replace those that may have been blocked in the process of pursuing those goals. Hope has been shown to be applicable and to relate to performance in various domains, including the workplace (Youssef & Luthans, 2007).

The above definitions tie hopeful thinking expressly to goals. By focusing on goal objects, we are able to respond effectively to our surrounding environment. Snyder et al. made the distinction between high-hope people and low-hope people. Compared to the vague and ambiguous nature of the goals for low-hope people, high-hope persons (Snyder et al., 1998) are more likely to conceptualize their goals clearly.

In addition to setting goals for conflict resolution, hope theory would encourage professionals and clients to set goals that "stretch" the clients (Snyder, 2002). In hope theory, goals that are difficult enough to be challenging, but easy enough to be accomplished are called "stretch goals." Such goals encourage the clients not only to "patch up" conflicts, but also to grow as an individual. For example, a stretch goal might be to increase well-being or connectedness, instead of just resolving the conflict. Continuously setting and meeting stretch goals is a way to move oneself toward a more positive, strengths-based stance.

Hope theory is considered a member of the *positive psychology* family, as mentioned in Chapter 1, along with optimism and self-efficacy: the power of believing you can. As an example of hope theory and self-efficacy theory, we have seen the importance of "The Audacity of Hope" and "Yes, we can," used by Barack Obama to become President of the USA. Hopeful thought reflects the belief that one can find pathways to desired goals and become motivated to use those pathways. Hope serves to drive the emotions and well-being of people.

Hope can be seen as a journey. Three components are needed: a destination (goal), a road map (pathways), and a means of transport (agency). It is a thought process that taps a sense of agency and pathways for one's goals. The pathway component involves a person's belief that one can set goals and devise multiple ways to reach them. Both short-term and long-term goals should be of value and be challenging but attainable. Once goals are set, a person's thoughts are focused on the ability to plan ways to reach these goals. When a route to a goal becomes blocked, those who are more hopeful devise alternate ways to pursue them. If a goal is permanently blocked, high hope people set a substitute goal that is satisfying.

The agency component involves the person's conviction that one has the inner determination to implement plans, even when faced with obstacles. Successful steps on the pathway towards a goal fuel a person's inner determination that, in turn, propels further progression towards the goal. To have a high hope level, a person must activate both components.

Goals are the first component of hope. They are the mental targets of human action. There are four categories of hopeful goals:
- Approach goals (moving toward a desired outcome);
- Forestalling negative outcome goals (deterring or delaying unwanted occurrences);
- Maintenance goals (sustaining the status quo);
- Enhancement goals (augmenting an already positive outcome).

Research shows that setting goals of moderate certainty characterizes high hope, while it probably enhances hope because it increases motivation. When goals are perceived to be too difficult or too easy, people likely do not try as hard to reach them.

Pathway thinking is the second component of hope. It reflects the routes that people produce in relation to goals. Pathway thinking involves the perceived capacity to come up with mental road maps to reach goals. It is a way to link the present to the future through one's goals. Research on athletes shows that sports performance is increased when individuals envision the sequence of steps necessary to perform well. High hope people are more skilled than low hope people at creating a detailed primary route to goal attainment. They are also better able to produce alternative routes to goals when those primary routes are impeded.

Agency thinking is the third component of hope. The ability to generate adaptive goals and perceived pathways will not result in actual goal attainment, unless the individual also has sufficient motivation to implement those routes. Agency thinking involves thoughts about one's ability to initiate and sustain movement along pathways toward desired goals, even when faced with impediments. Related to this point, there is evidence that high hope individuals show a greater preference for agency-affirming statements than low hope people: "I will find a way to get this done." or "Yes we can!" A key difference is between the words *can* and *will*, with the former pertaining to the capacity to act and the latter indicating intentionality to act.

Hope theory is built upon goal-pursuit thinking. Positive emotions (see broaden-and-build theory later in this chapter) flow from perceptions of successful goal pursuit. Blockages to pathways or agency may impair coping. Negative emotions are the product of unsuccessful goal pursuits and undermine well-being. The perceptions of unsuccessful goal pursuit can stem from insufficient agency and/or pathway thinking or the inability to overcome a thwarting circumstance. So goal-pursuit cognitions cause either positive or negative emotions.

High hope individuals will find it easier to generate alternative pathways when the original pathway is blocked than low hope individuals. Another finding is that high hope people, as compared to low hope people, have coping advantages when their goal pursuits are unimpeded, as well as when they are impeded (Snyder, 1994; Snyder et al., 1998). High hope people also learn to anticipate difficulties as a natural part of life and therefore are more resilient to stressful experiences. Another observation is that high hope people naturally break big goals into small subgoals. Small steps can lead to big changes, so setting frequent short-term "stepping-stone" goals is important. The three components of hopeful thinking – goals, pathways and agency – are so intertwined that the elicitation of any one should ignite the entire process of hopeful thought. Research also showed that optimism and hope are highly and positively correlated.

In the now classic "Robbers Cave Experiment," Sherif et al. (1961) demonstrated that arbitrary role assignments could produce socially constructive as well as deleterious effects. In the summer of 1954, Sherif set out to demonstrate that within the space of a few weeks, he could bring about two sharply contrasting patterns of behavior in a sample of normal eleven-year old boys. First, he would transform them into hostile, destructive, antisocial gangs; then, within a few days, change them again, this time to become cooperative, constructive workers and friends concerned about and even ready to make sacrifices for each other and for the community as a whole. To produce friction between the two groups of boys, a tournament of games was arranged: baseball, touch football, a treasure hunt, and so on. The tournament started in a spirit of good sportsmanschip, but as it progressed good feeling soon evaporated.

Before undertaking the task of turning hatred into harmony, Sherif wanted to demonstrate that, contrary to the views of some researchers of human conflict, mere interaction, pleasant social contact between antagonists, would not reduce hostility. The hostile boys were brought together for social events like going to the movies and eating in the same dining room. Far from reducing conflict, these situations only served as opportunities for the rival groups to berate and attack each other.

Conflict was finally dispelled by a series of stratagems. Sherif arranged to interrupt the water pipes coming from a tank about a mile away. He called the boys together to inform them of the crisis and both groups volunteered to search the water line for trouble. They worked together harmoniously and before the end of the afternoon, they had located and corrected the difficulty. On another occasion, when everyone was hungry and the camp truck was about to go to town for food, it turned out that the engine would not start, and the boys had to pull together to get the vehicle going.

According to Sherif the critical element for achieving harmony in human relations is *joint activity on behalf of a superordinate goal*. Sherif: Hostility gives way when groups pull together to achieve overriding goals which are real and compelling for all concerned" (p. 58).

The Greek philosopher Aristotle (2004) cites the archer as his favorite example in describing moral wisdom. An archer comprehends his task if, first, he knows what his target is and, second, he is aware of all circumstances (the means) that determine the situation in which he has to shoot. He has assessed the strength and direction of the wind, the characteristics of the arrow, and the tension of the bow. Aristotle sees the wise person as such an archer, someone with knowledge of the target (the goal) and of the means to reach the goal (the pathways). The archer is more likely to hit the right mark if he has a target to aim at. Aristotle stated that striving for excellence is important. Knowledge of the goal is therefore only useful if there is a striving to attain that goal (agency).

Csikszentmihalyi (1997) describes the *flow* experience: The experience of enjoyment, a positive universal mental state that cuts across cultural, gender, and age differences. It is about the sense of concentration, a complete immersion in what one is doing. There is also a sense of control (or actually not thinking about the possibility of losing control). One tends to forget oneself and there is a feeling of transcendence and a distortion of the sense of time. Csikszentmihalyi states that people report clarity of goals as the condition that makes such experiences possible: Failing to plan is planning to fail. Another condition is the immediacy of feedback. To keep focused concentration, people need to know how well they are doing. And, finally, people feel what can be done and what one can do are in balance.

Broaden-and-Build Theory of Positive Emotions

Little attention has so far been paid to theories of positive emotions in psychology and conflict management. This may well reflect the spirit of the age in which most disciplines have focused on problems and it may also reflect the nature of emotions themselves. The literature in psychology for the last 30 years has 46,000 papers about depression and only 400 papers about joy (Meyers, 2000).

Positive emotions are fewer in number than negative emotions, generally a ratio of three to four negative emotions to one positive emotion are identified (Meyers, 2000). Positive emotions are less differentiated than negative emotions and this imbalance is also reflected in the number of words in most languages that describe emotions. The broaden-and-build theory (Fredrickson, 2003) suggests that positive emotions (interest, contentment, enjoyment, happiness, joy, pride, relief, affection, love) broaden one's awareness and encourage novel, varied, and exploratory thoughts and actions. Over time, this broadened behavioral repertoire builds skills and resources. For example, curiosity about a landscape becomes valuable navigational knowledge; pleasant interactions with a stranger become a supportive friendship; aimless physical play becomes exercise and physical excellence.

This is in contrast with negative emotions, which promote narrow, immediate survival-oriented behavior. Positive and negative emotions are different in their links to action. For example, the negative emotion of anxiety leads to the specific fight-or-flight response for immediate survival. To survive, we immediately focus our attention on a specific behavioral response such as running or fighting, and therefore we do not expand our thinking to other behavioral alternatives. Positive emotions, on the other hand, do not have any immediate survival value, because they take one's mind off immediate needs and stressors. However, over time, the skills and resources built by broadened behavior enhance survival.

Fredrickson believes that it is this narrowing effect on our thought-action repertories that distinguishes negative and positive emotions. When we are experiencing negative emotions that accompany problems or conflicts, our attention narrows and we limit our behavior repertoire. This does not offer solutions; we feel "stuck." The usual approach of trying to find solutions by delving further into the problem or conflict perpetuates the situation by creating more negative emotions that continue to narrow our attention and further the sense of "stuckness."

Fredrickson proposes that, in contrast to negative emotions that narrow our thought-action repertoires, positive emotions broaden our thought-action repertoires and build enduring personal resources physically, intellectually, psychologically, and socially.

People who are feeling positive show patterns of thought that are more flexible, unusual, creative, and inclusive. Their thinking tends to be more efficient and more open to information and options. It is suggested that positive emotions enlarge the cognitive context, an effect recently linked to increases in brain dopamine levels.

The broaden-and-build theory is an exploration of the evolved function of positive emotions and has substantial support. Fredrickson has conducted randomized controlled lab studies in which the participants were randomly assigned to watch films that induce positive emotions such as amusement and contentment, negative emotions such as fear and sadness, or no emotions. Compared to people in the other conditions, participants who experience positive emotions show heightened levels of creativity, inventiveness, and "big picture" perceptual focus. Longitudinal intervention studies show that positive emotions play a role in the development of long-term resources such as psychological resilience and flourishing. Individuals who express or report higher levels of positive emotions show more constructive and flexible coping, more abstract and long-term thinking, and greater emotional distance following stressful negative events.

Fredrickson (2000) found that positive emotions also serve as particularly effective antidotes for the lingering effects of negative emotions, which narrow an individual's thought-action repertoires. In other words, positive emotions have an *undoing effect* on negative emotions because positive emotions are incompatible with negative emotions. Additionally, to the extent that a thought-action repertoire (i.e., specific action tendency) narrowed by negative emotion evokes physiological changes to support the indicated action, a counteracting positive emotion, and the consequently broadened thought-action repertoire, should quell or undo this physiological preparation for specific action. By returning the body to baseline levels of physiological activation, positive emotions create physiological support for pursuing the wider array of actions called forth.

Positive emotions have a unique ability to down-regulate the lingering cardiovascular aftereffects of negative emotions. Beyond speeding physiological recovery, the undoing effect implies that positive emotions should counteract any aspect of negative emotions that stems from a narrowed thought-action repertoire. For instance, negative emotions can influence people toward narrowed lines of thinking consistent with the specific action tendencies they trigger. When angry, individuals may dwell on getting revenge or getting even; when anxious or afraid, they may dwell on escaping or avoiding harm; when sad or depressed, they may dwell on the repercussions of what has been lost.

Fredrickson's positivity ratio (2009) – comparing positive and negative thoughts, emotions and activities during our day to day lives – shows a tipping point in the ratio around the 3:1 mark, where people experience transformed lives through positivity. For those with positivity ratios below 3:1, positivity is inert and useless; for those with ratios exceeding 3:1, positivity forecast both openness and growth. "Only those people truly enjoyed the sweet fruits of positivity" (p. 135).

In sum, focusing as soon as possible on developing a win-win situation (game theory), focusing on positive goals (quantum mechanics and neuroscience), focusing on hope and what difference it would make if the things hoped for would become reality (hope theory), and, finally, focusing on positive emotions (broaden-and-build theory) all help to create an atmosphere in which the conflict can be transformed into something positive: the preferred future of our clients.

Story 2: Feeding a Fellow

A woman died, and on her journey on to the next life, she found herself stand-ing in an amazingly elaborate banquet hall. The walls were lined with the most expensive timbers, crystal chandeliers hung from the high ceilings, and original paintings of all the great masters decked the walls. A huge banquet table ran through the center of the hall and was loaded with every possible delicacy and the most awarded of the world's wines. 'This must be heaven' she thought, a little surprised. She didn't believe she had led a life so good or holy as to deserve such a reward. Undeterred, she eagerly raced to her place at the table, dropping into her chair and then noticed something dreadful.

Both her arms were in splints. She could not bend her elbows. Her hands felt like they were at the end of a distant pole. She had no trouble taking hold of the luxurious delicacies that lavished the table but was unable to maneuver them to her mouth. As she paused to look beyond what she had initially, and greedily, desired for herself, she saw other people sitting around the table. Their arms were also in splints, they cursed, grew angry, became frustrated, and cried, but it seemed that nothing could save them from their fate.

'I was wrong' thought the woman. 'This is not heaven but hell. I wonder what heaven is like.' Her wish transported her into another, identical banquet hall. Similar expensive chandeliers hung from the ceilings. Original artworks by all the great masters were on the exotic wooden walls. A similar carved wood-en table stretched down the center of the hall. It was equally laden with every imaginable exotic dish and award-winning wine. Again, she eagerly rushed to her seat hoping to share in the delicacies. Then again she perceived the same unnoticed fact: her arms were still in their rigid splints.

About to despair, she looked around the table. There was something very different about this group of diners who all appeared happy and well-fed. She looked at their arms, which, like hers, were bound in splints, but her fellow guests were jovial and communicative in spite of their confinement. At last, she finally saw what made the difference. They were not struggling to bend immov-able arms, not greedily trying to force food into their own mouths. Instead, each person would pick up a delicacy politely requested by the person opposite him or her. Rather than seeing the restriction as a disability, they used it to benefit their fellow diners. Having secured an item of food, they reached across the table to feed the other person. She found that in giving to another, she gained. Others fed her, just as she fed them. 'This is not just about food' she thought, for as the people shared food, they also shared conversation. They exchanged stories, spread feelings of optimism, and joined in an experience of joyfulness, 'Yes' she decided, 'this is heaven.'

In the next chapters you will see how the focus on setting clear goals, thus enhancing hope, is used to invite clients to think and talk about their hopes for the preferred future instead of focusing on the conflict they are facing: "What is your hoped for outcome?", "What are your best hopes?", or "What difference would that make?" It permits people to concentrate their energy on improving the future rather than dwelling on problems of the past. Designing pathways to achieve this hoped for outcome (goal) is another important component of solution-focused conflict management, since people need to know what the pathways to their goals are in order to achieve them. Motivating clients to become their own agent for change and giving feedback to clients at the end of every session are other elements highlighted in solution-focused conflict management.

3 Solution-Focused Interviewing

Every problem is an opportunity in disguise
Benjamin Franklin

Principles of Solution-Focused Interviewing

The solution-focused model in psychotherapy was developed during the 1980s by De Shazer, Berg, and colleagues at the Brief Family Therapy Center in Milwaukee, USA. They expanded upon the findings of Watzlawick, Weakland, and Fish (1974), who believed that the attempted solution would sometimes perpetuate the problem and that an understanding of the origins of the problem was not always necessary.

The propositions of De Shazer (1985) are:
- The development of a solution is not necessarily related to the problem (or conflict). An analysis of the problem itself is not useful in finding solutions, whereas an analysis of exceptions to the problem is.
- The clients are the experts. They are the ones who determine the goal and the road to achieving this. De Shazer (1994) assumes that problems (or conflicts) are a sort of subway tokens: They get the person through the gate (to the table of the mediator) but do not determine which train he will take, nor do they determine which stop he will use to get off.
- If it is not broken, do not fix it. Leave alone what is positive in the perception of the clients.
- If something works, continue with it. Even though it may be something completely different from what was expected.
- If something does not work, do something else. More of the same leads nowhere.

Story 3: Do Something Different

A Japanese costal village was once threatened by a tidal wave, but the wave was sighted in advance, far out on the horizon, by a lone farmer in the rice fields on the hillside above the village. There was no use in shouting and there was no time to go home to warn his people. At once he set fire to the field, and the villagers who came swarming up to save their crops were saved from flood.

Looking to the Future (1)

Psychiatrist Milton Erickson contributed to the development of solution-focused interviewing: He asked students to read the final page of a book and then to speculate on what had preceded. In the same vein, solution-focused interviewing begins from the perceived goal of the clients. Erickson also emphasized the competence of the clients and considered it necessary to search for possibilities for action (and change) revealed by the clients (Rossi, 1980).

Erickson also used the technique *pseudo-orientation in time.* He asked his patients to envision that they would meet him again in six month's time. They would imagine that their problems were over and how they managed to do so. And although his patients did not always use the exact solutions they told him in the beginning, many patients stated that they were doing better.

In solution-focused literature, Frankl (1963) is often cited as an example of *posttraumatic success* (Bannink, 2008d). He says of his stay in a German concentration camp that a prisoner who no longer believed in the future – his future – was doomed. He describes an incident where he staggered along in a row of prisoners on his way to the work area, in the cold and without food. He forced himself to think about something else. Suddenly he saw himself standing on the stage of an auditorium where he was giving a lecture about the psychology of the camp system. In this way, he succeeded in lifting himself above the suffering of the moment and was able to view the torment as if it already were in the past. His focus on the future saved him for that moment. And this vision of the future even became reality, as after the war he conducted many successful lecture tours.

> Begin with the end in mind ... To begin with the end in mind means to start with a clear understanding of your destination. It means to know where you're going so that you better understand where you are now and so that the steps you take are always in the right direction (Covey, 1989, p. 98).

The importance of looking to the future will be explored further in Chapters 4 and 6.

Assumptions With an Eye on Solutions

Selekman (1993) gives a number of pragmatic solution-focused assumptions. They offer professionals a new lens for looking at their clients.

The term resistance is not useful. It suggests that the client is not willing to change and that the professional is detached from the treatment system. Also de Shazer (1984) states that resistance is not a useful concept. It is preferable to approach each client in a cooperative manner rather than from a position of resistance, power, and control. The professional uses the client's strong points, resources, words, and opinions and asks competence questions.

Change is a continuous process; stability is an illusion. The question is not whether, but when, change will occur. The client can be helped in making positive self-fulfilling prophecies. A direct relation appears to exist between talking about change and the actual result. It is helpful to talk about successes in the past, present, and future. Collecting information about past and present failures, however, often leads to negative outcomes.

As soon as the client is invited to notice and value small changes (the exceptions), that person will begin to expect other changes to take place and will start believing in the snowball effect. Often the beginnings of a solution already lie in the client, but remain unnoticed. These are the exceptions to the problem (hidden successes). Inquiring into the exceptions gives insight into which positive actions could happen to a larger extent or more often; inquiring into hypothetical solutions also gives insight into the direction of the search. Because the client is the expert and finds the solutions himself, they suit him and are compatible with his situation and are found quickly and will endure. Solution-focused professionals maintain a nonpathological view on people. Generally people have or have had one or more difficulties in their life. These may have become chronic, depending on the way in which the client or those around him (including therapists) react. The client possesses resources and competencies that can be drawn on. As a result, hope and self-confidence can be rebuilt.

Walter and Peller (2000) give three solution-focused questions that invite their clients to relate their success stories:

- How did you do that?
- How did you decide to do that?
- How did you manage to do that?

The first question derives from the assumption that the client has done something and therefore supposes action, competence, and responsibility. The second question derives from the assumption that the client has taken an active decision, affording him the opportunity to write a new life story with influence on his own future. The third question invites the client to relate his successes.

Watzlawick et al. (1974) state that *problems are unsuccessful attempts to resolve difficulties.* They name three ways in which the client may unsuccessfully deal with his problems: Action is necessary, but client does nothing (denial of the problem); action is undertaken, but it is not necessary or necessary to a lesser extent (client follows a diet that is so strict he cannot possibly maintain it); action is undertaken on the wrong logical level. For instance: a client requests someone else to behave spontaneously. This is impossible because, upon complying with the request, it is no longer a spontaneous action.

The basic assumption in solution-focused interviewing is that *no problem is always there to the same extent* and that, to solve it, *not a great deal about the problem needs to be known.* The professional may investigate what the client is doing differently when the problem is not there, or there to a lesser extent, or what is different about those times when it ceases to be a problem for a while.

The client defines the goal for treatment. It is important to receive from the client a very precise and detailed description of what his life will look like once his goal is reached. Einstein believed that *our theories determine what we observe.* Reality is observer-defined and the professional participates in co-creating the system's reality. A psychoanalytical therapist will probably see unsolved conflicts and psychological deficits. It is impossible for professionals to not have a theory. Solution-focused professionals are co-authors who help the clients rewrite their problem-saturated story. De Shazer (1984) sees professional and client as tennis players on the same side of the net; the professional is not an observer on the sidelines.

Finally, there exist *no definitive explanations or descriptions of reality.* There are many ways to look at a situation, all equally correct. Professionals should not be too attached to their own preference models: Nothing is more dangerous than an idea, if it is the only one you have (see Chapter 14).

■ Exercise 1

Look around the space where you are right now and find five objects that are beige. If you have found five beige objects, before you list them, say quickly which blue objects you saw. Probably you did not see any blue objects or just a few and you have to look again to find more blue objects.

This exercise makes clear how clients see their conflict situation. They will describe it as beige: They don't want beige, they suffer from it, they might even hate beige. By asking clients what they want instead of beige (e.g., blue), they can begin to focus on blue as a better alternative to beige: "What would a blue life look like?", or "When are or were there already pieces of blue?", or "On a scale where 10 means a totally blue life, and 0 means a totally beige life, where would you say you are right now?"

You can do this exercise with your clients if they describe the conflict as always present or when you want to clarify your approach as a solution-focused mediator. One last question: What do you as a professional have to know about beige to be able to look with your clients for blue?

Acknowledgment and Possibilities

O'Hanlon (1999) states that when someone is not happy or is not getting desired results, that person has to do something different. Einstein states in the same vein, that insanity is doing the same thing over and over again and expecting different results. Therefore, the client has to change *the doing of the problem* or *the viewing of the problem*, or both. In changing the doing of the problem, the focus is on the concrete actions someone can take to make these changes by doing two things (O'Hanlon, 1999, p. 53):

- Pay attention to repetitive patterns that the person is caught up in, or others with the person are caught up in, and change anything possible about these patterns.
- Notice what actions are being taken when things are going better, and do more of those.

In changing the viewing of the problem the focus is on changing how a person thinks and what that person pays attention to as a way to change the situation for the better. This can involve five things:

- Acknowledge feelings and the past without letting them determine what the person can do.
- Change what the person is paying attention to in a problem situation.
- Focus on what the person wants in the future rather than on what the person does not like in the present or the past.
- Challenge unhelpful beliefs about self and the situation.
- Use a spiritual perspective to help the person transcend troubles and draw on resources beyond usual abilities.

In summary: Solution-focused interviewing is about balancing acknowledgment and possibilities for change.

From a *social-constructionist perspective* (Cantwell & Holmes, 1994), consideration is given to how the mediator can contribute to the creation of a new reality for the clients. The capacity of the clients for change is connected to their ability to begin seeing things differently. These shifts in observation and definitions of reality occur particularly in the conversation on the desired future and usable exceptions. The solution-focused questions are intended to define the goal and the solutions, which (for the most part) are assumed to be already present in the clients' lives. The questions that make a difference relate to the manner in which the clients are managing despite their problems, to what they think is already going well and should persist, and to what has improved since making the appointment. Questions regarding goal formulation, exceptions, scaling, and competencies extract the relevant information. Here, a different layer of the client is tapped, which usually remains unexplored in problem-focused conversations. The mediator is not the expert with all the answers, but is informed by the clients, who create their own solutions. The mediator is expert in asking solution-focused questions (Bannink, 2006c, 2010a) and in motivating behavioral change by relating to the motivation of the clients (see Chapter 8).

Microanalysis of Conversations

Tomori and Bavelas (2007) use *microanalysis*, the close examination of the moment-by-moment communicative actions of psychotherapists. They micro-analyzed demonstration sessions by experts on solution-focused and problem-focused client-centered therapies, like Steve de Shazer and Carl Rogers. The first analysis examined how the therapist communicated, namely, whether the therapist's contribution took the form of questions or of formulations (e.g., paraphrasing). The second analysis rated whether each question or formulation was positive, neutral, or negative. Results showed that the solution-focused and client-centered experts differed in how they structured the sessions: The client-centered therapists used formulations almost exclusively, that is, they responded to client's contributions. Solution-focused experts used both formulations and questions, that is, they both initiated and responded to client contributions. They also differed in the tenor of their contributions: the solution-focused therapists' questions and formulations were primarily positive, whereas those of the client-centered therapists were primarily negative and rarely neutral or positive.

Positive therapist content includes question, statements, formulations or sug-gestions by the therapist that focus the client on some positive aspect of the cli-ent's life (e.g., a relationship, trait, or experience in the past, present, or future). Positive client content includes questions, statements, formulations, or sugges-tions by the client that focus on some positive aspect of life (e.g., a relationship, trait, or experience in the past, present, or future). Negative therapist or client content is the opposite of positive content. Another finding is that, when the therapist's utterance is positive, clients are more likely to say something posi-tive, whereas when the therapist's utterance is negative, clients are more likely to say something negative.

Microanalysis can complement outcome research by providing evidence about what therapists do in their sessions. Focusing on language as the tool of mediation has not yet been done. Comparing the language of problem-fo-cused and solution-focused mediators might generate the same findings as in the microanalysis of psychotherapy.

Empirical Evidence

In solution-focused psychotherapy there are a growing number of outcome stud-ies. Unfortunately, these outcome studies are not yet available for solution-fo-cused conflict management, but one might expect the results to be similar.

When determining the effectiveness of psychotherapy it is important to not only register progress on arbitrary metrics, but also to monitor improvement on points that the client himself finds relevant (Kazdin, 2006). He argues for the addition of clinical relevance: the client himself should determine whether in his daily life he has found the treatment useful.

De Shazer (1991), De Jong and Berg (1997), Miller, Hubble, and Duncan (1996) all carried out studies regarding the success of solution-focused psychotherapy. However these studies are not controlled studies (they are one group pre-post studies) and, hence, cannot be considered satisfactory evidence. Gingerich and Eisengart (2000) gave an overview of 15 outcome studies in which they distinguished between statistically well-monitored and less well-monitored research. One of the statistically well-monitored analyses demonstrated that solution-focused psychotherapy yields results comparable to those of interpersonal psychotherapy with depressed students. These outcome studies are generally small sample studies, conducted by investigators with allegiance to solution-focused psychotherapy.

Stams et al. (2006) conducted a meta-analysis of 21 international studies including 1,421 clients to achieve quantitative evidence for the efficacy of solution-focused psychotherapy. They examined client characteristics, type of problem, characteristics of the intervention, form of the study, and factors that might affect publication bias. They found that although it does not have a larger effect than problem-focused therapy, it does have a positive effect in less time and satisfies the client's need for autonomy. Macdonald (2007) states that studies have shown that, for all models in psychotherapy, central issues for effective therapy include client-therapist collaboration in a therapeutic alliance with an emphasis on clear goals.

Six randomised, controlled trials show benefit from solution-focused therapy, with three showing benefit over existing treatment. Fourteen of fifteen comparison studies show results as good or better then "treatment as usual," while one is equivocal. Effectiveness data are available from 30 studies including more than 2,200 cases with a success rate exceeding 60% and using an average of 3–5 sessions of therapy time. Two meta-analyses appear to confirm these findings on the information so far available. There are at least 30 other smaller published studies. Solution-focused therapy is a realistic and practical approach to many problems in mental health and elsewhere.

Research shows that all therapeutic models work, but that solution-focused conversations require less time, not only for clients, but also in training the professional.

Thus solution-focused therapy can claim to be the equal of other psychotherapies, while also taking less time and resources for treatment, reducing the strain placed on therapists and providing help for a number of groups and clients who have previously found it hard to obtain useful help from psychological therapies (Macdonald, 2007, p. 113).

Finding an equal benefit for all socio-economic classes is important, since this contrasts with other approaches to psychotherapy, which are more effective for those from higher socio-economic and educational groups.

Indications and Contraindications

The solution-focused model has proven to be applicable in all situations where there is the possibility of a conversation between a client and a professional, in (mental) health care (De Shazer, 1985, 1994; De Jong & Berg 1997, O'Hanlon & Rowan, 2003; Bannink, 2005, 2006c, 2006d, 2007a, 2007b, 2007c, 2008d; Bakker & Bannink, 2008), in management and coaching (Cauffman, 2003; Berg & Szabo, 2005; Furman & Ahola, 2007), in solution-focused organizations (Stam & Bannink, 2008), in education (Metcalf, 1995; Goei and Bannink, 2005), in working with people with mental retardation people (Westra & Bannink, 2006; Roeden & Bannink, 2007a, 2007b) and in mediation (Bannink, 2006a, 2006b; 2008a, 2008b, 2008c, 2008e, 2008f, 2009c, 2009d, 2010b). The solution-focused model is suitable for use with individuals, in groups or teams, and in organizations, where it is important that there is a shared goal: their preferred future (or that clients are able to envision one during the meetings).

A *contraindication* is a situation in which it is impossible to establish a dialogue with the client, for example, if a (mandated) client is psychotic or does not want to talk to a professional. Another contraindication concerns a solution-focused conversation that has yielded disappointing results. In these situations, a lengthier form of more problem-focused contact might be indicated, or another solution-focused professional might be appointed. Research shows that the relationship with the professional is far more important for a successful outcome than any method (Norcross et al., 2002).

A different contraindication does not concern the clients, but the attitude of the professional or the institution. If the professional is not inclined to let go of his attitude as an expert, giving advice to the client, solution-focused interviewing will not work. The final contraindication relates to professionals or institutions maintaining waiting lists for reasons of financial security. Solution-focused interviewing is mainly short in nature, as a result of which waiting lists can be reduced relatively quickly.

Story 4: The Problem of Looking for Problems

During the French revolution an attorney, a physician and an engineer were sentenced to death. When the day of their execution arrived, the attorney was first onto the platform that supported the guillotine. He stood tall and proud, uncompromising of his principles. 'Blindfold or no blindfold?' asked the executioner. The attorney, not wanting to be seen as fearful or cowardly in the face of death, held his head high and answered 'No blindfold'. 'Head up or head down?' continued the executioner. Still there would be no compromise. 'Head up' said the attorney proudly. The executioner swung his axe, cleanly severing the rope that held the razor-sharp blade at the top of the scaffold. The blade dropped swiftly between the shafts and stopped just half an inch above the at-

torney's neck. 'I am sorry' said the executioner. 'I checked it just this morning, like I always do. This should not have happened.'

The attorney seized on the opportunity. Although willing to die for his principles, he preferred to live. 'I think' he addressed the executioner, 'if you check The procedural Manual For Execution By Guillotine, you will find there is a clause that states that if the guillotine malfunctions, the condemned is permitted to walk free'. The executioner checked his manual, found the attorney to be correct, and set him free.

The doctor was the next to be led to the platform. 'Blindfold or no blindfold?' asked the executioner. 'No blindfold' said the doctor as proudly as the attorney. 'Head up or head down?' asked the executioner/ 'Head up' said the doctor standing tall and defiant. The executioner swung his axe, cutting the rope cleanly. Once again the blade stopped just half an inch above the doctor's neck. 'I can't believe this' exclaimed the executioner. 'Twice in a row! I checked it out thoroughly this morning, but rules are rules and I have to abide by them. Like the attorney, your life has been spared and you may go.'

The engineer was the third to mount the stand. By this time, the embarrassed executioner had double-checked the guillotine and everything looked operational. 'Blindfold or no blindfold?' he asked the engineer. 'No blindfold' came the reply. 'Head up or head down?' asked the executioner. 'Head up' said the engineer. For the third time, the executioner swung back his axe to slash the rope that supported the blade. Just as he was about to bring the blow forward and severe the line, the engineer called out 'Stop! I think I can see the problem.'

4 Solution-Focused Conflict Management

Most people see what is, and never see what can be
Albert Einstein

Four Dimensions in Conflict Thinking

At the same time that De Shazer published his book Keys to Solution, De Bono (1985) published a book called Conflicts: A Better Way to Resolve Them. There are some remarkable similarities in the two books, although both say they never met. De Bono distinguished four dimensions in conflict thinking: Is the action *fight, negotiate, problem solve,* or *design?*

In the fighting approach, words of this idiom are used: It revolves around tactics, strategy, and weak points. This is the language of the courtroom, where winning is the goal. The word party, as often used in mediation, also stems from this idiom and in solution-focused conflict management is replaced by the neutral word client.

Negotiating suggests a compromise, whereby the possibilities are limited to what already exists, rather than envisaging something new (see Einstein, 1954).

Problem solving concerns the analysis of the problem along with its causes (the medical or mechanical model). A disadvantage of problem solving is that when the problem is defined, the type of solution expected is also defined. With these three ways of thinking about conflict one looks backward at what already exists.

The fourth and best way in conflict resolution, the *design* approach, looks forward at what might be created. One possibility is to first imagine and determine the end point and then to see what solutions mayget us there. Another approach is to simply jump to the end and conceive a *dream solution.* Its content can be illogical, because it concerns a fantasy. More importantly, it can suggest circumstances in which the conflict would no longer exist, "Imagine the conflict resolved. What would you then be doing differently?" Hypothetical questions are useful, because they refer to alterations in the condition of the conflict ("Suppose there is a solution, what difference would that make?"). Perceptions and thinking have become locked solid; therefore, there is a need to introduce some instability in order to unfreeze the thinking. The basic purpose of the mediator is to convert a two-dimensional fight into a three-dimensional exploration leading to the design of a desirable outcome. "Conflict thinking should not be a fight but a design exercise." (De Bono, 1985, p.124).

Looking to the Future (2)

Beckhard and Harris (1987) developed a model of planned change in organizations:

Current state → Transition state → Desired future state

It often helps to develop a deeper understanding of the process and the phases of planned change. The first step for those involved is to envision a desired future state. This helps to establish a goal for the change and serves the purpose of beginning the process of unfreezing, as well as being open to something different. It has been found that starting with what people desire in the future generates energy, enthusiasm, motivation, and commitment to the plan and its implementation (Lindaman & Lippitt, 1979, as cited in Beckhard & Harris, 1987).

Once this is undertaken, the next step is to move backwards and assess the current state of the organization or entity, its current capabilities, capacities, and so forth. After the envisioned future, and assessment of current state, the next phase is to create a transition state. This is based, in part, on the gaps between the current state and the desired future state. These gaps create tension, which serve as a motivating force in the transition state. The transition state is a way for a system to balance or modulate its own need for stability with its need for change. Although this model is most often used in large, complex organizational change, the concepts are applicable on both the individual and small-group levels.

Salacuse (1991) mentions some rules to ensure that clients are "paddling the same canoe in the same direction." Precisely define the goal of the negotiations and investigate new possibilities for creative solutions that serve the interests of all clients. Emphasize the positive aspects of the goal and the relationship, stressing those moments when agreements are (already) reached and when progress is (already) being made. Salacuse (2000) also discusses the importance of having a vision of the end result. Michelangelo could already see in a block of marble the magnificence of David, as Mozart already heard in his quiet study the overpowering strains of the Requiem. What clients seek is not just help but help with their future: "Whether an advisor is a doctor, a lawyer, a financial consultant or a psychotherapist, his or her mission is to help the client make a better future" (Salacuse, 2000, p. 44).

Mnookin et al. (2000) note that lawyers and clients are so focused on wanting to be in the right that they tend to overlook solutions possibly lying outside the field of the original conflict. Frequently, these solutions have nothing to do with the formal conflict (compare with De Shazer: The development of a solution is not necessarily related to the problem) and the agreement may be of an order that could never be envisaged in a courtroom. Furthermore, they state that lawyers (and clients) all too often despair of there being a possible positive outcome, and as a result do nothing.

Haynes, Haynes, and Fong (2004) state that a mediator can only mediate in the future tense. They propose that a mediator uses future-focused questions to initiate change.

> Most clients are highly articulate about what they do not want and equally reticent about what they do want. However, the mediator is only useful to the clients in helping them to determine what they do want in the future and then helping them decide how they can get what they want. It is difficult for the mediator to help clients not get what they do not want, which is what clients expect if the mediator dwells with them on the past (Haynes, Haynes, & Fong, 2004, p. 7).

Coleman (2000) describes an important tradition of the Mohawks, the native peoples of Quebec. This tradition makes it the responsibility of the chiefs to think in terms of seven generations. It is based on the belief that the decisions made seven generations ago affect people today, and that the decisions made today will affect the next seven generations. Unfortunately, says Coleman, this type of long-term thinking about conflicts, although essential, is uncommon in the work of scholars and practitioners of conflict resolution. There are, however, a few exceptions. One of them is focused social imaging, a creative and hopeful process for working with disputants who are stuck in the web of malignant social conflict. The approach is quite simple. They actively involve participants who have a conflict (such as Arab and Israeli youths). They begin by identifying some of the shared social concerns regarding the conflict (such as reducing community violence or improving community health services). The participants are then asked to temporarily disregard the current realities of the situation and to step into the future. They are asked to put themselves into a future approximately twenty or thirty years from the present, in which their concerns have been effectively dealt with. As the participants begin to develop some sense of the social arrangements and institutions in this idealized future, discussion ensues. Together, they begin to create a vision for a community that has the institutions and relationships necessary to effectively address their shared concerns. Then the participants are asked to move slowly backward in time, and to begin identifying the steps that would precede establishment of such institutions and relationships. This is both a creative and a critical process of examining the achievement of their ideal future in the context of the circumstances that are likely to exist between the present and such a future. Ultimately, this process results in both a vision and a plan for making the vision reality. It can also serve to open up the participant's awareness of options and approaches to the current conflict that they previously found impossible to image.

Bunker (2000) describes a large-group method: the *future search*.

> Then there are activities that ask people to dream about their preferred future in the face of the reality they now confront. Finally, there is work to agree on the best ideas for future direction, and action planning to begin to make it happen. Although the overall plan is rational, the activities themselves are interesting, fun, and challenging. The interactions that occur among people create energy and motivation for change (p. 550).

When there are differences about the future, the key is the search for common ground; people are asked to focus their minds and energy on what is shared. People are encouraged to notice and take differences seriously, but not to focus on, or give a lot of enery to, conflict resolution. Rather, they try to discover what they agree on, and this becomes the base for moving forward.

Clients, Parties, Lawyers, and Litigants: What's in the Name?

In this book the term *clients* is used to refer to the participants in the mediation. Some may call these participants *litigants* or *parties*. Since these terms stem from the fighting idiom, as described above, the more neutral term *clients* is preferable from a solution-focused point of view. Lawyers involved in mediation are not called clients in this book, although they may refer their clients to the mediator.

■ Exercise 2

Think back to a period in your life when you had a problem or a conflict. How did you resolve these difficulties then? Think of at least three things that you did that were helpful.

If you currently have a problem or conflict, which of those former ways could you apply again (or are you already applying) to the current situation? And what do you know about the ways in which other people resolved a similar problem or conflict?

Differences Between Traditional and Solution-Focused Conflict Management

Table 1 provides an overview of the differences between traditional conflict management and solution-focused conflict management. A more elaborate comparison between traditional models (the problem solving model, the transformative model, and the narrative model) and the solution-focused model is given in Chapter 14.

There are three main differences between traditional conflict management and solution-focused conflict management. The first difference is the *focus*. In traditional conflict management, the focus is on the conflict, the causes, the

Table 1 Differences between traditional and solution-focused conflict management

Traditional conflict management	Solution-focused conflict management
Past/present-oriented	Future-oriented
Conversations about what clients do not want (the conflict).	Conversations about what clients do want instead of the conflict (their preferred future).
Focus on exploring and analyzing the conflict.	Focus on exploring and analyzing the exceptions to the conflict.
Conversations about the same and impossibilities	Conversations about differences and possibilities
Conversations for insight and working through conversations about blame and invalidation	Conversations for accountability and action. No invitations to blame and invalidation. Insight may come during or after mediation.
Clients are sometimes seen as not motivated (resistance)	Clients are seen as always motivated (although their goal may not be the goal of the mediator)
Client is sometimes viewed as incompetent (deficit model)	Client is always viewed as competent, having strengths and abilities (resource model)
Mediator gives advice to client; he is the expert	Mediator asks questions; clients are the experts. Attitude of the mediator is "not-knowing" and "leading from one step behind"
Mediator's theory of change	Client's theory of change
Expression of affect is goal	Goals are individualized for all clients and do not necessarily involve expression of affect
Recognition and empowerment are goals	Recognition and empowerment can be means to reaching the preferred future
Interpretation	Acknowledgment, validation, and opening possibilities
Big changes are needed	Small changes are often sufficient
New skills have to be learned	Nothing new has to be learned: clients are competent and have made changes before
Feedback from clients at end of the mediation	Feedback to and from clients at the end of every session in mediation
Long-term conflict management	Variable/individualized length: often short-term conflict management
Mediator indicates end of sessions	Clients indicate end of sessions
Success is defined as the resolution of the conflict	Success is defined as reaching the preferred outcome, which may be different from (or better than) the resolution of the conflict

impact, the emotions, and so on. In solution-focused conflict management, the focus is on what clients want different in their lives and how to make that happen. The focus is on the preferred future of the clients involved, "What do they want instead of the conflict?" Conversations are about what clients do want instead of what they do not want. Of course, the impact the conflict has on the clients is acknowledged, but this is very different from focusing on the conflict and its consequences. The second difference is the fact that the development of solutions is not necessarily related to the conflict. Therefore, an analysis of the conflict itself is not useful in finding solutions.

The final difference is the *attitude of the mediator*. In solution-focused conflict management, the attitude of the mediator is *not knowing* (the mediator asks questions) and *leading from one step behind* (the mediator does not give advice; see also Chapter 3: Microanalysis of Conversations).

Solution-focused mediators try to work in ways that allow clients to be the experts about their own experiences and what these mean. They think the best way to lead clients is the solution-focused way of leading from one step behind. They adopt a posture of not knowing and develop interviewing skills that allow clients to provide information about themselves and their situation. They do not pull or push, they are not leading. Clients are considered the experts of their own lives and the mediator asks questions to invite clients to inform him and to come up with their own solutions to the conflict. This attitude promotes client trust, confidence, and hopefulness about the future.

Changing Conflict Stories

There are four types of conflict stories that can be changed to solution stories using solution-focused conflict management. These conflict stories are:

- Blame stories, in which someone gets the blame for the conflict;
- Impossibility stories, in which change is seen as impossible in a given situation;
- Invalidation stories, in which someone's feelings, desires, thoughts or actions are seen as wrong or unacceptable;
- Nonaccountability stories, in which people are excused from responsibility for their actions by claiming that they are under the control of other people or some other factor that is beyond their control.

Conflict stories can be changed to solution stories by acknowledging the impact of the conflict and the facts of the situation instead of evaluating, judging, or explaining it. Counterevidence can be found that contradicts the unhelpful conflict stories and your clients can be reminded that whatever story they have, that story is not all there is to them. Creating compassionate and helpful stories and finding a kinder, gentler view of themselves, the other, and/or the situation is also helpful (O'Hanlon, 1999).

Chapter 3 already demonstrated how solution-focused interviewing is about balancing acknowledgment and possibilities for change. In solution-focused conflict management, the role of the mediator is to acknowledge the impact of the conflict and to help the clients to focus on possibilities for change instead of impossibilities. In doing so, persuasion and influence are always present (see Chapter 8).

One of the challenges mediators face is seeing a case from others' perspectives. In solution-focused conflict management, the process is seen from a different perspective than is typical in other forms of mediation. In this model, the conflict is considered from the perspective of the clients and what goal *they* want to achieve, rather than from the perspective of the mediator, the evidence, or the likelihood of success at trial. This approach offers a new and broad perspective from which to see options for resolution. It is about finding the *win-win scenario* (see Chapter 2), where clients are asked what they would consider to be a win and the mediator helps them create that goal.

Lazarus (2000) developed and researched a model of how individuals react to stressful events. His research indicated that when the event is viewed as a threat, people tend to use wishful thinking, avoidance, hostility, and aggression as coping strategies. When the stressful event is seen as a challenge, then they are more likely to seek solutions and thoughtful action because of their perception.

The Chinese character for *crisis* is pictured below. Crisis (Wei Ji) means danger *and* chance. You could tell your clients about this Chinese wisdom and ask them the following solution-focused questions:

- Suppose you see not only threat or danger in the conflict, but also the challenge or chance, what challenge or chance would you see?
- Suppose you take that challenge or chance, what would be different?
- What would you be doing differently?
- How would that be helpful?
- How would that change your relationship with the other(s)?
- What do you need to be able to see the situation from that point of view?

5 Four Basic Solution-Focused Questions

People are generally better persuaded by the reasons, which they themselves discovered than by those, which have come into the minds of others
Blaise Pascal

■ Exercise 3

Which question do you usually ask at the beginning of a mediation? Do you opt for a *problem-focused* question such as, "What is the conflict about?" or "What are your difficulties?" Do you opt for a neutral question like, "What brings you here today?" Do you opt for a question that implies that you are going to work hard, "What can I do for you?" Do you ask a *solution-focused* question to find the goal of the clients for the mediation. A solution-focused question is, "What is your best hope?" or "What would you like to have achieved at the end of this mediation?" or "How would you know you don't have to come back because things are better?" or "What would you like to have instead of the conflict?"

Do you ask a solution-focused hypothetical scenario like the *miracle questions*: "Suppose a miracle happens during the night, and the conflict that brought you here is (sufficiently) solved, but you were unaware of it. What would be the first thing in the morning that would tell you that something had happened during the night? How would you notice? What would be different? What would you be doing differently? What else? Who would be the next person to notice that things have changed? How could they tell? What would they be doing differently? How would your relationship with these people change?" Try all these possible questions and notice the differences in the reactions of your clients and the differences in the atmosphere of the conversation.

Questions about Hope

The four basic solution-focused questions are as follows:

1. What are your best hopes?
2. What difference would that make?
3. What is already working in the right direction?
4. What would be the next step/next sign of progress?

The first basic solution-focused question is about *hope*. As already described in Chapter 2, hope is like a journey: a destination (goal), a road map (pathways), and a means of transport (agency) are needed. Research on the subject of hope has shown that it is important to have a goal and ways to reach that goal. Hopeful people have a clearer goal (destination) than nonhopeful people. They also have a clearer image of the route by which they can reach their goal; they have a mental map. Additionally, they believe that they themselves can do something to get closer to their goal (they are their own means of transport). And, should the route to the goal be blocked, high-hope persons will think of an alternative more easily and will continue to feel better than low-hope persons. Therefore the first question in solution-focused conflict management, after establishing rapport and explaining the rules of play, is, "What are your best hopes?" or "What is your desired outcome of this mediation?" The mediator makes sure he invites all clients involved to think and talk about their hopes for a better future.

Offering a vision that change is possible and that there are new and better ways to deal with the situation is important in conflict management. Solution-focused conflict management fits well with this value, because solution building is about the development of a well-formed goal through asking about client's best hopes and what differences those would make or by asking the miracle question or other projections in time (see Chapter 6). Those questions encourage clients to develop a detailed vision of what their lives might be when their conflict and problems are solved. The emphasis is on inviting clients to create the vision by drawing on their own frames of reference. It relies less on practitioner suggestions than do problem solving approaches. It fosters hope and motivation in clients and promotes self-determination.

Solution-focused conflict resolution also counters any tendency to raise false hope in clients. They define their own visions for change and, as experts on their own situation, clarify what parts of the preferred future (or the miracle) can and cannot happen. They think and explain what is realistic and what is not.

Cloke (2005) uses questions about hope and the preferred future "to expand heart spaces in mediation:"
- What do you hope will happen as a result of this conversation?
- Why is that important to you?
- What kind of relationship would you like to have with each other?

Questions about hope are different from questions about expectations. The question, "What do you expect from this mediation?" invites participants to look at the mediator for the solution of their conflict. The risk might be that they see you as the only means of transport to reach their goal instead of themselves. If a person wants to (re)gain a glimmer of hope, even in crisis situations, ask the following questions:

- What helped in the past, even if only marginally?
- How do you cope with everything that is going on and all you have gone through?
- How do you succeed in getting from one moment to the next?
- Could it be worse than it is? Why is it not worse?
- What else do your important others say you do well in very bad times?
- Imagine that in 10 or 15 years, when things are going better, you look back on today, what will have helped you to improve things?
- On a scale of hope (10 = very hopeful and 0 = not hopeful at all), where would you say you are right now? What is in that mark? Why is not lower?
- Suppose you were one or two marks higher, what would be different in your life? What would you be doing differently? What would be different in your relationship with the other client(s)? What would they be doing differently?
- Suppose there is a solution, what would be different and, more specifically, better?

Story 5: The Power of Hope

A severely ill man was in hospital. The doctors had given up any hope of a recovery. They were unable to ascertain what the man was suffering from. Fortunately, a doctor famous for his diagnostic skills would visit the hospital. The doctors said that maybe they could cure him if this famous doctor was able to diagnose him. When the doctor arrived the man was almost dead. The doctor looked at him briefly, mumbled moribundus (Latin for dying) and walked over to the next patient. A few years later the man – who did not know a word of Latin – succeeded in finding the famous doctor. 'I would like to thank you for your diagnosis. The doctors had said that if you were able to diagnose me, I would get better.'

Questions About Differences

The second basic solution-focused question is, "What difference would that make?" Asking this question invites clients to describe their preferred future in positive, concrete, and realistic terms. Many will say that they will feel relieved, at rest, relaxed, or happy when they describe their preferred future. How would they react and how would they interact? What would their day look like? What would they be doing differently, so others would know that the clients have reached their preferred future?

Mostly this preferred future will be described without the conflict that brought them to the mediation table, although some clients describe their preferred future with the conflict still present, but without it bothering them as much.

Bateson (1972) wrote about the importance of differences.

> But what is a difference? A difference is a very peculiar and obscure concept. It is certainly not a thing or an event. This piece of paper is different from the wood of this lectern. There are many differences between them – of color, texture, shape, etc. But if we start to ask about the localization of those differences, we get into trouble. Obviously the difference between paper and the wood is not in the paper; it is obviously not in the wood; it is obviously not in the space between them; and it is obviously not in the time between them. Difference which occurs across time is what is called change. A difference, then, is an abstract matter (Bateson, 1972, p. 452).

De Shazer (1991) states that it is difference itself that is an important tool for professionals and clients. It is not simply that there are differences that make a difference. In and of themselves, differences are just differences, they do not work spontaneously. Only when recognized can they be put to work to make a difference. "In the language game of therapy, the client's story makes the therapist see things one way: The therapist's revision (a difference) makes the client see things another way" (p. 156). The professional needs to find a point or element in the client's story that allows for a difference being put to work. There are many possible points where a distinction can be marked, places where a difference can be pointed to. Any of these differences might be put to work toward making a difference so that the client can say that life is more satisfactory.

Change is happening all the time and our role is to find useful change and amplify it. Since solution-focused conflict management is about change and helping clients to make a better future (Salacuse, 2000), questions about positive differences are considered very important. What difference would it make when your best hopes become reality? How would your future look? What would you be doing differently? How would your relationship with the other person(s) differ? What would they be doing differently (Bannink, 2010)?

Asking about exceptions to the conflict is another way of asking about differences. When the conflict was there to a lesser extent, what was different? What were you doing differently and what was the other person doing differently? How was your relationship different then? Questions about exceptions can be very useful because they may reveal what was working in times when the relationship was better. Some things that were helpful in the past may be used to improve the relationship. Also, scaling questions (see below) may help to find differences that make a difference. Scaling questions can be asked about progress, pre-session change or hope, motivation, and confidence.

If you always do what you have always done
You will always get what you've always got
So for a change do something different
And do something different for a change
Mark Twain/Anon.

Case

In mediation in a divorce case, the mediator says to both clients, "Here is a different kind of question, one that puts things on a scale from 10 to 0. Let's say that 10 equals how your life would be if all was going very well, and 0 equals how bad things were when you made the appointment to see me. Where are you on that scale today? Where would you like to be at the end of this mediation?"

Questions About What Is Already Working

The third basic solution-focused question is, "What is already working in the right direction?" The mediator may start by asking for presession change. Most clients have tried other ideas before seeing a mediator. The mediator can inquire whether changes already occurred before the first meeting. It is a common assumption that clients begin to change when the professional starts to help them with their conflict. But change is happening in all clients' lives. When asked, two thirds of clients in psychotherapy report positive change between the moment they made the appointment and the first meeting.

Exploration of presession change can reveal new and useful information. When clients report that some things are already better, even just a little bit, the mediator may ask *competence questions* like, "How did you do that? How did you decide to do that? Where did you get this good idea?" When asked about what is already working in the right direction, exception-finding questions are frequently used. Those questions are new to many clients, who are more accustomed to problem-focused questions. When asked about exceptions, they may start noticing them for the first time. Solutions are often built from formerly unrecognized differences.

Wittgenstein (1968) states that exceptions already lie on the surface, you don't have to dig for them. The aspects of things that are most important to us are hidden because of their simplicity and familiarity. We are unable to notice something, because it is always before our eyes. The mediator, having heard and explored these exceptions to the conflict, then compliments the clients for all the things they have already done. Exploration of exceptions is similar to other aspects of solution-focused conflict management in that it respects the client's frame of reference.

A scaling question can then be used: "On a scale where 10 indicates that you have reached your preferred future, and 0 indicates the worst situation you can imagine, where would you say you are right now?"

By means of a scaling question, a mediator can help clients to express complex, intuitive observations about their past experiences and estimates of future possibilities. Scaling questions invite clients to put their observations, impressions, and predictions on a scale from 10 to 0. For example, you may ask a client, "On a scale from 10 to 0, where 10 means you are confident that you both can reach a solution in this mediation, and 0 means you are not confident at all, where would you say you are now?"

Scaling questions can be used for many purposes. They can be used to access the client's perception of almost anything, like presession change, confidence, motivation, hope, investment in change, and evaluation of progress. First asking for details about exceptions and then asking a scaling question will usually generate a higher mark on the progression scale than when the mediator first asks a scaling question and then asks what exceptions have contributed to that mark.

Questions About the Next Step or Sign of Progress

The fourth and last basic solution-focused question is either, "What would be your next step?" or "What would be a sign of progress?" By asking, "What would be *your* next step, the mediator invites each client to – for the first time in some mediations – actually think about what they themselves can do to ameliorate the situation instead of waiting for the other(s) to do something." Of course this question is only asked when clients want to go further on the scale of progress. When the current state is the best possible state at that moment, then the conversation can continue by asking clients how they could maintain the status quo.

Notice that in those two questions, it is still left open who will take the next step. When appropriate, the mediator asks, "What can you do yourself and what do you need from the other(s)?" Sometimes this question opens the eyes of clients that they themselves can (and should) contribute to improving the situation, instead of just waiting for what the other person(s) will do. The question about the next sign of progress is still more open as to who should do what and when (Bannink, 2007a). A sign of progress may also be something that could happen without the clients taking action.

The four basic solution-focused questions can be seen as *skeleton keys*: keys that fit in many different locks. You don't have to explore and analyze each lock (e.g., problem or conflict) before you can use these keys.

Case

During a mediation session about parental access to children after a divorce, Mr. wishes to bring the meeting to a halt. The mediator asks him, "Suppose you were to continue, what could be *your first small step* that would enable you to continue?" Mr. states again that he wants the mediation to stop and the mediator asks again, "I know you wish to stop the mediation, but suppose you would like to continue, what could be the first small step?" Mr. says he doesn't know. The mediator then asks a relationship question (see Chapter 6), "Imagine we were to ask your children, what would they suggest as a first small step to take for there to be progress?" Mrs. replies immediately that the children would clam up if they were asked anything. The mediator asks, "Imagine your children wouldn't clam up. What would they suggest might be the first small step?" Mr. replies that they might say that they would like to have some fun together, like going to a park or eating a hamburger.

Mr. and Mrs. like this idea and, after some encouragement from the mediator, they make arrangements there and then to go to the park and playground, weather permitting, or otherwise to go for a hamburger. The mediator compliments them both on this plan and asks them to keep the conversation lighhearted while they are with the children. If that proves to be too difficult, they are asked *to act as if* things are going normally, in the best interest of their children.

Solution-Focused Conflict Management in Practice

Asking the first question. Following introductions, an explanation of solution-focused mediation, and a presentation of the structure and rules of play, the mediator asks, "What needs to come out of this mediation?" or "What are your best hopes?" Clients may react to this with a (brief) description of the conflict, to which the mediator listens with respect, or they may indicate their goal for the meeting. In solution-focused conflict management, it is important to both acknowledge the facts and influences of the conflict and to help clients change the situation. It may be helpful to give clients one opportunity to say what definitely needs to be said at the start of the mediation. This reduces the possible continued reverberation of negative emotions (see Chapter 10).

Developing a clearly formulated goal. Clients are invited to describe what will be different once the conflict is resolved, "What difference would it make if your hopes have come true? Sometimes the *miracle question* is put forward, "Imagine a miracle occurring tonight while you sleep that would (sufficiently) solve the conflict that brought you here, how would you notice in the morning that this miracle had taken place? What would you be doing differently? What would be different between you? How would the miracle manifest itself during the day?" Compare this with De Bono's *dream solution*. Goal examples are a (restored) good cooperation within the team, a positive relationship between two or more people, or the ending of a relationship in as good a manner as possible. If no mutual dependency can be found and no mutual goal can be formulated, mediation is not indicated. The courtroom may then be a good alternative.

Solution-focused conflict management revolves around designing the clients' best case scenario or better case scenario. Sometimes, a good case scenario or a good enough case scenario is more realistic. The worst case scenario is only used when clients are not (yet) prepared to look at their preferred future. In that case, the worst case scenario may be a good alternative, hoping that clients will be motivated to change when they imagine the costs caused by further escalation of the conflict (see the escalation ladder in Chapter 6).

Assessing pre-mediation change. Sometimes clients report gains prior to the formal initiation of mediation. Shining a spotlight on change illuminates already existing client resources and allows their enlistment. Of special interest is what clients have done to bring about this change (see Chapter 6). The mediator may ask, "Many clients notice that, between the time they call for an appointment and the first session, things already seem different. What have you noticed about your situation?"

Assessing motivation to change. The mediator assesses the relationship with each client: Does it concern a visitor, a complainant, or a customer relationship?

In a visitor relationship, the client is mandated and does not attend of his own volition. He has been referred by others (judge or manager of an organization) and does not personally come forward in search of help. Those referring the client are concerned or have a conflict with him. The mediator will attempt to create a context in which the client may voluntarily ask for help. That may involve, for example, asking what those referring the client would like to see different in the future and to what extent the client is prepared to cooperate in this.

In a complainant relationship, the client is suffering emotionally, but does not (yet) see their part in the conflict and/or the solutions. The other team members, management, or the system are to blame and need to change. The mediator will acknowledge the client's suffering and may give suggestions for reflecting upon, analyzing, and observing moments when the conflict is or was there to a lesser extent or moments when (an element of) the miracle or desired outcome is already happening.

In a customer relationship, the client does see their part in the conflict and/or solutions and is motivated to behavior change. Solution-focused conflict management goes beyond the verification of commitment: The mediator is trained in relating to the existing motivation and in stimulating change.

It often happens that clients will start mediation from a visitor or complainant relationship. This early assessment of each client's level of motivation is of essential importance for the strategy of the mediator and for the type of homework suggestions (see Chapter 8).

Exploring the exceptions. Questions are asked regarding the moments when the conflict is less serious and who does what to bring these exceptions about; the mediator can also ask about moments that already meet (to a degree) the goal of the clients, "What is already working in the right direction?" The exceptions to the conflict may be positive, times when the conflict is or was less serious, or may be negative, times when the conflict is or was worse. Clients may be invited to do more of the positive exceptions and less of the negative ones.

Utilizing competence questions. The mediator looks for the clients' competencies through questions such as, "How did you do that?" or "How did you decide to do that?" or "How did you manage to do that?" The answers can foster empowerment and may be of help in revealing whether something that has helped at an earlier stage can be done again.

Utilizing scaling questions (10 = very good, 0 = very bad). Scaling questions will be asked so the mediator may assess improvements between the moment when the appointment was made and the end of the first mediation session. These questions also serve to measure and speed up progress in the mediation, to measure and stimulate motivation and confidence, or to inspire hope that the preferred future can be reached: "If, on a scale, 10 means *pure collaboration,* the ideal outcome, and 0 means *pure conflict,* where would you say you are right now?" (Schelling, 1960)

Feedback at the end of the session. At the end of the meeting the mediator formulates feedback for the clients, which contains compliments and usually some homework suggestions. The compliments emphasize what clients are already constructively doing to reach their goal and can be seen as a form of positive reinforcement of desired behavior. The suggestions indicate areas requiring attention by the clients or further actions to reach their goal. Also using client feedback to inform the mediatior invites clients to be full and equal partners in all aspects of mediation. Giving clients the perspective of the driver's seat instead of the back of the bus may also enable them to gain confidence that a positive outcome is just down the road (see Chapter 12).

Evaluating progress. There is regular evaluation of how far clients have come in achieving their hoped for outcome. They explore what is yet to be done before they would consider the mutual goal (sufficiently) reached and would deem the mediation process complete (usually finalized with a settlement agreement). What would be the next step? What would be the next sign of progress? Every solution-focused conversation is considered the final one; at the end of every conversation the mediator asks whether another meeting is considered necessary. Clients will determine the scheduling of the next meeting.

Maintaining an attitude of not knowing and leading from one step behind. The mediator stands behind the clients and asks solution-focused questions, inviting them to look at their preferred future and defining steps to get there. Clients are considered to be the experts about their own experiences and what these mean: They can provide the necessary information about themselves and their situation.

For a protocol of the first meeting see Appendix 1.

■ Exercise 4

First, talk for five minutes with another person about a personal problem of your own – an irritation, concern, or conflict. You ask the other person to respond in a problem-focused way. This includes questions like, "How long has this been going on?" "What do you feel?" "How bad is it?" "What else is wrong?"

Then you talk again for 5 minutes about the same problem and now you ask the other person to react in a solution-focused way. This includes questions like, "What would you like to have instead of the problem?" "When are there moments when the problem is less?" The person could also ask, "What are you hoping for? What difference would that make? What else?"

Notice the differences between the two conversations. Some might say the tone of the conversation is lighter and more optimistic in the solution-focused conversation. Some might say the problem is already solved in the few minutes of the solution-focused conversation. Some might say that they loved the problem-focused questions because they did not have to think hard and in the solution-focused conversation they did.

You can reverse roles: now you are the listener and the other person relates a personal problem. First, you react for 5 minutes in a problem-focused way and then five minutes in a solution-focused way. Again notice the differences in the two short conversations.

6 More Solution-Focused Questions

> *The world of reality has its limits*
> *The world of imagination is boundless*
> Jean-Jacques Rousseau

More Questions

More solution-focused questions are presented in this chapter. These questions are used to find more details about anything that is useful (what else), invite clients to look at their situation from different perspectives (interactional matrix), and help clients to step into a future where the conflict is no longer there (future-oriented questions). Scaling questions for hope, motivation or confidence, or respect and collaboration can be used to help clients simplify complex matters and find out where they are and where they would like to be. Finally, the question, "What is better?" is important because this is the opening question in all subsequent meetings.

What Else?

The question, "What else?" implies that the mediator knows that there is more to come. It is different from questions like, "Is there something else?" Clients often respond to this simple question by giving more information and ideas than they thought they could. "What is your best hope?" "What else?" And, again, "What else?"

The mediator continues asking this question until the client responds by saying, "This is about it," or "Don't you think this will do?" The mediator is always complimentary of the efforts of the clients. The question, "What else?" invites clients to think outside their comfort zone: this is the moment when the most creative ideas are born.

■ Exercise 5

Think of something you would like to change in your own life. Ask yourself, "What difference would that make?" "What else would be different?" And, "What else?" And, again, "What else?" See how you will probably be able to come up with far more things than you imagined you would.

Case

There is a conflict between the head of the department (Mr. B) and an employee (Mrs. A). According to Mr. B, Mrs. A regularly arrives too late for work and leaves earlier than is officially allowed. This attitude disturbs Mr. B enormously, even more so because Mrs. A ignores his comments and doesn't change her behavior. Mrs. A claims to keep more or less to her work schedule. The conflict escalated after Mrs. A insulted Mr. B when he again complained about her behavior and attitude. Mrs. A has now ceased working pleading ill health. With Mr. B, there exists a complainant relationship. In his opinion, Mrs. A must change. With Mrs. A, there exists a visitor relationship because she claims that there is no problem.

In mediation, it emerges that Mrs. A does indeed have a goal; she would like her boss to stop his constant criticism of her. This expressed wish on her part now puts her in a customer relationship; she is prepared to make certain changes to her behavior to achieve this goal. Apart from questions about goal formulation, the mediator asks the following *relationship questions* (see below), "What do you think Mr. B could say that might make you do things differently so that he stops his critisism?" And, "What are you prepared to do to help to achieve an end to the critisism from your boss?" And, "What should replace his critisism? What would you like to have instead?"

Mrs. A replies that she would like to enjoy her working relationship as much as she did in the past. She would like to receive praise from her boss instead of critisism. Mr. B also expresses hope that their working relationship will improve, he is very tired of how things have been lately. One of the principles on which they agreee is to introduce shorter working hours, whereby Mrs. A can leave earlier in the afternoon in order to care for her sick mother. A new work contract is drawn up at the end of the meeting.

Premediation Change

The Greek philosopher Heracleitus (540–480 BC) is often credited with saying that nothing is permanent but change: "*Panta rhei.*" Exploring what is different about better versus worse days, times without conflict versus times when conflict seems to get the best of clients, can help mediators to use the description of such fluctuations as a guide to activity.

Studies in psychotherapy (Miller, Hubble, & Dunacan, 1997) show that 15–66% of clients experience positive, treatment-related gains prior to the formal initiation of treatment. Simply scheduling an appointment may help set the wheel of change in motion and present the possibility for an emergent story of competence and mastery.

Mediators may view their clients through a change-focused lens. Shining a spotlight on change, as solution-focused mediators do, illuminates existing client resources and allows their enlistment. The client is encouraged to make *before* and *after* distinctions. They should reflect upon their experiences and distinguish between the way they were and the way they are now. A change-focus requires that the mediator believe, like Heracleitus, in the certainty of change and create a context in which to welcome, explore, and develop new or different perspectives and behaviors. Of special interest is what the clients have done to bring about this change and how the clients make sense of it all. Solution-focused questions about pre-mediation change are:

- Since you made the appointment for this mediation and our meeting today, what is better?
- Many clients notice that, between the time they call for the appointment and the actual first meeting, things already seem different. What have you noticed about your situation?
- What is already different/better between you?
- How were you able to do that?
- What would you need to do (or what needs to happen) for you to experience more of that?
- As you continue to do these things, what difference will that make to you tomorrow? How will your day go better?
- What are these changes saying about you as a person?

Interactional Matrix

Relationship questions are used to invite clients to construct descriptions of interactional events as well as their meanings. The professional finds out who are the client's significant others and weaves them into the questions so as to encourage clients to describe their situations and what they want different in interactional terms. They are a good way to invite clients to amplify their solutions. A relationship question might be, "Suppose the two of you could get along a little bit better in the future, what would he notice you do instead of losing your temper?" or "What would your boss say will be different between the members of your team if things were somewhat better?"

Walter and Peller (1992) introduced the interactional matrix (see Appendix 3). This matrix is a tool for selecting questions to facilitate the building of solutions from an interactional view and to invite clients into areas of difference. Across the top of the matrix are the frames used in various parts of solution building. These are the frames of goal, hypothetical solutions (like the miracle question or other future-oriented question), and exceptions. Along the left side of the matrix are the different reporting positions of the question and response. The first is the *for self* position. Questions of this position invite clients to answer from their own position. The next position is *for the other*. Questions from this position invite clients to answer questions as if they were listening and reporting for someone else who is involved in the solution context. For example, in a divorce mediation, the ex-partners are asked what they think their children will say about certain solutions. To answer this question, the clients must suspend their own way of thinking for a moment and imagine the other(s) answering the question. They must put themself in the other's shoes briefly or at least think of what the other person might say in response to the question. This ususally induces a search for new and perhaps different information.

The third row of the matrix is reporting *for the detached* position. This position is for someone who is detached from the conflict and solutions and is merely observing: "If I were a fly on the wall observing you and your team members, what would I see you doing differently when things are better?" This question invites clients to answer from a neutral position. Each question or row of the matrix invites clients into an area of experience different from their usual way of thinking.

■ Exercise 6

Think of a situation where you have a problem or conflict with another person.

Ask yourself every question from the matrix or let someone else ask you these questions. Keep the same order as in the schedule: from goal to hypothetical solutions (miracle question) to exceptions. Notice the differences in your reactions and how this changes your personal film. Then, choose the next row with another viewpoint and notice again how this changes your reaction. What differences do you notice in your personal film? What questions make more difference or are more useful to you?

Case

During a mediation about a conflict at work, the employee Peter, head of administration for a nonprofit organization, expresses his belief that the working atmosphere is failing and beyond repair. He has no plans to return to work. Because of the situation, he has decided to stay at home and not attend the office, claiming sickness benefit.

For Peter, this is the first occasion on which he speaks of the conflict with both mediator and the board of directors of the organization. The mediator asks, "Suppose there might still be some way forward for you, what might be the first step that you could take or that others should take?"

The mediator asks some questions from the interactional matrix. They include:

- In what way would your colleagues perceive that you had taken a first small step?
- What would your spouse say about what you are doing differently? What would allow that person to say you are making progress?
- If I were a fly on the wall and I could see that there still remains a faint hope of the possibility of you returning to work, what differences in your behavior would I see?

■ Exercise 7

You can practice your solution-focused skills by asking your clients these questions from the interaction matrix:

1. When this conflict is resolved, what difference will you notice about the other person? What will he/she be doing differently? What else?
2. When this conflict is resolved, what will this other person notice is different about you? What will you be doing differently? What else?
3. When you are being watched by an outside observer, what will he or she notice that is different about your relationship with the other person? What will you be doing differently? What else?

Looking to the Future (3): Future-Oriented Questions

Dolan (1998) and Isebaert (2005) describe a number of ways in which clients are invited to look at themselves in or from the future. The ways involve *the letter from your future, the older and wiser version of yourself, one year later,* and *the five-year plan.* The technique *pseudo-orientation in time* and the technique of Covey to describe one's own funeral in three year's time were described in Chapter 3.

From experience we know that these interventions are only helpful for clients with whom a customer relationship exists and who are motivated to explore their preferred future. If there is still a visitor or complainant relationship with the client, other interventions are recommended. The technique of *consensus-building* (see Chapter 10) is also a form of projection into the future.

You can ask your clients to *write a letter from their future* to their current self. You can say the following, "Write a letter from the future to your present self. Pick a time in the future that is meaningful to you (six months, one year, five years). Then, imagine that you are doing well and explain in your letter what you are doing and where you are. Problems or conflicts that you are now struggling with are either resolved or you have found satisfying ways to cope with them. Give a description of the most important things you did to achieve this. How did you resolve difficulties and conflicts? What or who was most helpful? And finally give yourself some wise and compassionate advice."

■ Exercise 8

Write a letter from your future (6 month, 1 year) to your present self in which you look on the positive way you were able to solve the conflict you had. Keep the letter and read it again after the time (6 month, 1 year) has passed. You might be surprised!

Clients may be asked to imagine that, many years later, they are *an older and wiser version* of themselves. They are still healthy and have all intellectual capabilities. They may ask this older and wiser version of themselves questions like:

- If you look back on your life, what advice would you give to your younger version?
- If you look back on your life, what do you like most about the life you have lived?
- Is there anything you would rather have done differently?
- What do you hope your children will remember about their lives with you?
- On a scale from 10 to 0, with 10 being all wishes achieved and 0 being no wishes achieved, to what extent have you achieved your life's wishes?
- What would be the smallest step you can take to reach a higher mark?

Clients can also go for a walk with the older and wiser version of themselves and ask for advice in resolving problems or conflict.

The clients can be asked to describe a day, *one year from now*. The description may be detailed and indicate exactly what the client is doing during that day. If a client experiences difficulties in making a choice, this may be a useful intervention because the consequences of choices become clear in this way. Also, when the mediator has the impression that his client cannot foresee the consequences of a particular choice, this may be helpful.

In the *five-year plan*, the clients are invited to look further ahead than they usually do. They are asked to divide a piece of paper into boxes. On the vertical axis, possible (sub)goals that the clients want to achieve are written down. The goals can be about work, relationship, money, and so on. On the horizontal axis, the clients write where they would like to be in 5 years. Then, in the boxes, the clients write steps they can take to reach their goals. "If I want to be there in 5 years time, how far do I have to have come in three years? "What should I already have achieved? And in two years? One year? Three months? How can I start now?" The five-year plan helps clients formulate realistic goals and form a timetable to make them happen.

Story 6: Working from the Future Back

An English psychiatrist, named MacAdam, told this story.

A young girl I was working with had experienced abuse. She walked into my office...a very large girl with shaved hair, tattoos on her head and I don't think she'd showered in a week. I'd been asked to see her because she was so angry. She clearly didn't want to come and see an expletive-expletive shrink.

She'd been to a bunch of therapists before, social workers, psychologists and school counselors. I just said, 'You've talked to everybody about your past; let's talk about your dreams for the future.' And her whole face just lit up when she said her dream was to become a princess.

In my mind, I couldn't think of two more opposite visions, but I took it very seriously. I asked her about what the concept of princess meant to her. She started talking about being a people's princess who would do things for others, who would be caring and generous and a beautiful ambassador. And she described the princess as slender and well dressed. Over the next few months, we started talking about what this princess would be doing. I discovered that while this girl was 14, she hadn't been attending school for two to three years. She'd refused to go.

The princess she described was a social worker. So I said, 'Okay, it's now ten year's time and you've trained as a social worker. What university did you go to?' She mentioned one to the North of England and I asked, 'What books did you read... what did you study there?' She said, 'I don't know, Psychology and Sociology and a few other things like that.' Then I said, 'Remember when you were 14? You've been out of school for two or three years. Remember how you got back in school.'

She said, 'I had this psychiatrist who helped me.' And then I asked the important question: 'How did she help you?' And she started talking about how she made a phone call to the school and I followed-up: 'Who spoke? Did you or she?'

She replied, 'The psychiatrist spoke, but she arranged a meeting for us to go to the school.' 'Do you remember how you shook hands with that teacher when you went in? And how you looked and what you wore?' We went into these minute details about what that particular meeting was like, looking from the future back. She was able to describe the conversations they'd had, how confident she had been, and how well she had spoken.

About a month after this conversation, she said to me, 'I think it's about time we went to school, don't you? Can you ring and make an appointment?' I asked her if she needed to talk about it anymore and she said, 'No.' She knew how to behave.

When we went to the school, she was just brilliant.

I first met that girl about ten years ago. Now she's a qualified social worker. She fulfilled her dream, even though she attended a university different from the one she envisioned.

Scaling Questions: Hope, Motivation, and Confidence

Scaling questions about hope, motivation, and confidence can be used to find out how hopeful, motivated, or confident clients are that the mediation will be successful. These questions can be very useful at the start of mediation. Moreover, scaling questions are equally valid for the mediator, who can assess their own motivation, confidence, and hope. Questions for *scaling motivation* are:

- "If 10 means that you will do anything to reach your desired outcome and 0 means that you will just wait and see, at what point on the scale are you right now?"
- When your client gives a high score, for example 7 or 8, you may ask, "Where does this willingness to work hard come from?"
- When your client gives a low score, for example 2, you may ask, "How did you manage to reach 2, how come it is not 0 or 1?" The follow-up question could be, "What would 3 look like?" And, "What is required to move up one point on the motivation scale?"
- "Suppose you gave your motivation a higher score? What would you notice different about yourself? What would be different in your relationship with the other person?"

The mediator can also ask how *hopeful or confident* clients are that they will reach their preferred future:

- "If 10 means that you are completely confident that you will reach your hoped for outcome, and 0 means that you have no confidence at all, where on the scale would you say you are right now?"
- When your client gives a high score, you may ask, "You seem to be the type of person that, once a decision to tackle something has been made, has a strong belief that you will succeed?" or "Where does this high level of confidence (or hope) come from?"
- When your client gives a low score, for example 3, you may ask, "How did you manage to reach 3 despite the situation? What would one point up look like? What is needed to move up one point on the scale? What can you do yourself and what do you need from the other person?"

- "Suppose your confidence (or hope) was somewhat higher, what would you notice different about yourself? What would you be doing differently? What would be different in your relationship with the other person(s)?"

Case

Ms. A (employer) and Mr. B (employee) are at the table of the mediator. Mr. B says, "I do not think that this mediation will succeed; the former mediator has also not helped us much. We did make an agreement, but the implementation of what was agreed has never come off the ground. It has only led to more arguments and, on top of that, I can not work anymore." The (overoptimistic) mediator ignores this remark (even though Mr. B repeats that it should be up to the judge to make a decision) and, before long, the mediation reaches a deadlock. The mediator would have done better to validate the doubts of Mr. B by asking scaling questions with respect to his confidence and hope. Then, there might have been an opening to increase his confidence and hope. "Suppose you had a bit more hope, what difference would that make?" Also, the mediator could have asked, "How, despite your earlier experience, do you manage to sit here at the table?"

Scaling Questions: Respect – Contempt

In conflicts, mutual respect is often reduced to a minimum. Clients no longer see each other as a person – a subject, but as an object. Once the other was seen as a subject, maybe even with compassion, but they have now become an obstacle. Everything would be better if the other was no longer there. The other person is, in this way, always seen as less.

Only when someone stops seeing the other person as an object, may there be a turning point in the conflict, as any mediator knows. Only then can equality and reciprocity return. To address the topic of respect, the mediator may ask the clients a scaling question about respect and contempt:

- If 10 means that you have all possible respect for the other(s), and 0 means you have no respect at all, where would you say you are right now?
- Why is it not less?
- What mark would you like to reach in the future, since you will continue having contact with each other?
- What is already working in the right direction?
- What would be a next step or sign of progress?

The risk of being sued for malpractice seems to have very little to do with how many mistakes a professional makes. Analysis of malpractice lawsuits shows that there are highly skilled doctors who get sued a lot, and doctors who make lots of mistakes and never get sued. In other words, patients do not file lawsuits because they have been harmed by shoddy medical care. Patients file lawsuits because they have been harmed by shoddy medical care and *something else* happening to them.

The medical researcher Levinson (Gladwell, 2005) recorded hundreds of conversations between a group of physicians and their patients. Roughly half of the doctors had never been sued and the other half had been sued at least twice. Levinson found that, solely on the basis of those conversations, she could find clear differences between the two groups. The surgeons who had never been sued spent more than three minutes longer with each patient than those who had been sued (18.3 minuten versus 15 minutes). They were more likely to make "orienting" comments such as, "First, I will examine you, and then we will talk the problem over," which helps patients get a sense of what the visit is supposed to accomplish and when they ought to ask questions. They were more likely to engage in active listening, saying things such as, "Go on, tell me more about that." And, they were far more likely to laugh and be funny during the visit. Interestingly, there was no difference in the amount or quality of information they gave their patients; they did not provide more details about medication or the patient's condition. The difference was entirely in *how* they talked to their patients.

Psychologist Ambady listened to Levinson's tapes, zeroing in on the conversations that had been recorded between surgeons and their patients. For each surgeon, she picked two patient conversations. Then, from each conversation, she selected two ten-second clips of the doctor talking, so she had a total of forty seconds. Then, she removed the high-frequency sounds from speech that enable us to recognize individual words. What is left is a kind of garble that preserves intonation, pitch, and rhythm, but erases context. She found to her surprise that by using only those ratings, she could predict which surgeons got sued and which ones didn't. The judges of the tapes knew nothing about the skill level of the surgeons or how experienced they were, what kind of training they had, or what kind of procedures they tended to do.

They did not even know what the doctors were saying to their patients. All they were using for their prediction was their analysis of the surgeon's tone of voice. In fact, it was even more basic than that: If the surgeon's voice was judged to sound dominant, the surgeon tended to be in the sued group. If the voice sounded less dominant and more concerned, the surgeon tended to be in the nonsued group. Malpractice sounds like one of those complicated and multidimensional problems, but in the end it comes down to a matter of *respect*, and the simplest way that respect is communicated is through tone of voice, and the most corrosive tone of voice that a doctor can assume is a dominant tone. These interesting findings may well apply to other professionals, like mediators.

Scaling Questions: Pure Collaboration – Pure Conflict

Schelling (1960) asks, "If the zero-sum game is the limiting case of *pure conflict*, what is the other extreme? It must be the *pure collaboration* game in which the players win or lose together, having identical preferences regarding the outcome." In such a game, it is important that the players understand each other to discover patterns of individual behavior that make each player's actions predictable to the other; they have to test each other for a shared sense of pattern or regularity and to exploit cliches, conventions, and impromptu codes for signaling their intentions and responding to each other's signals. They must communicate by hint and by suggestive behavior. Two vehicles trying to avoid collisions, two people dancing together to unfamiliar music, or members of a guerrilla force that become separated in combat have to concert their intentions in this fashion, as do the applauding members of a concert audience, who must at some point agree on whether to press for an encore or taper off together.

Scaling questions along the dimensions of pure collaboration and pure conflict can be helpful to find out where clients are on the scale of collaboration and what they are hoping for. These questions can be very useful, especially when there will be an ongoing relationship in the future as in divorce cases, and cases involving neighbors or families. The same kind of questions that can be used for respect and contempt (see above), can be used here.

Glasl (1977) developed a model of escalation in conflicts: the *escalation ladder*. He imagines the escalation process, not as an ascending ladder, but as a descending one. Each new level of escalation restricts the options for action of the clients involved. The escalation process is seen as a process of successive closings of alternatives for action and the opening of new, although restricted, ones. On the individual level, this restriction of alternatives for action corresponds to a cognitive and moral regression.

The three phases of escalation can be described as follows. In phase one, the clients are aware of the existence of tension and conflicts of interests, but are still attempting to find a solution by means of communication. The conflict can be described as a problem and the behavior is oriented toward cooperation. From the point of view of game theory (see Chapter 2), the game is still a win-win game.

In phase two, tension is generated not just by the conflict itself, but also by the manner of interaction and relationship between the clients. The issues at stake in the conflict expand and, at the same time, the reciprocal perceptions change to the point where stereotypes develop. Mistrust and lack of respect between clients prevent direct communication. Cooperation-based strategies are abandoned and clients are primarily interested in enforcing their own interests, even against the other(s). The conflict can be described as a fight. The game shifts to a win-lose game.

In phase three, the actual conflict recedes into the background and its place is taken by the negative relationship between the now hostile clients. The prime goal now is not to enforce their own interests, but to destroy or damage the other(s). There is now a complete lack of respect or dignity. The conflict can now be described as a war. In the end, further intensification of the conflict can even end with fanatic self destruction. The game has now shifted to a lose-lose game.

The escalation ladder can be used as a scale when talking with clients about their conflict. The mediator may ask, "Where are you now on this scale? And what would happen if you do nothing? What would happen if you were one or two marks further down the ladder (if possible)? What will be the costs and what are the dangers?" With this, the hope is that clients will come to realize that the costs of further deterioration will be too great. From there on, clients are invited to consider the possibilities of de-escalation. This form of using scaling questions – first detailing the consequences of a worst case scenario – can also be applicable to conflicts where neither client is prepared to compromise by taking the first step toward a better future.

A positive form of escalation can be found when clients start building solutions to reach their goal. Escalation should therefore be about their preferred future, not about their past. I call this the best-case scenario. A nice way of doing this is to ask your clients, "What difference would that make? And what difference would *that* make? And what difference would *that* make?"

Feedback

At the end of every solution-focused meeting, the mediator constructs messages for the clients that include compliments and usually some suggestions. The compliments emphasize what clients are already doing that is useful in resolving the conflict and making a better future for themselves. The suggestions identify what clients could observe or do to further solve their conflict. Feedback is based on information that the clients have revealed in the conversations about their goals and exceptions to the conflict. Feedback focuses on what clients need to do more of or need to do differently to enhance their chances of success in meeting their goal.

Some professionals take a short break of about 5 minutes before giving the clients feedback. In that case, mentioning the break and the purpose of the break at the beginning of the meeting is advisable. Clients readily accept the rationale for the break if the mediator explains that he will use the break to think about all the things the clients have talked about and to formulate some feedback he hopes will be useful to them.

Feedback from the mediator could go like this, "I am impressed that you are both here today even though this was not your idea. It has not been easy to sit here today and face each other......talking about difficult matters too........ I would like to give you a suggestion.......Is that all right with you? Between now and the next time we meet, I would like you to observe what happens in your relationship that you want to continue, so that next time we meet you can tell me about it."

Clients can be asked to think of a suggestion for themselves during the break that they think might be useful in their situation as well. In addition, clients can give feedback to the mediator. They can be given the Session Rating Scale (SRS) at the end of every session (see Chapter 12/Appendix 5).

What Is Better?

Subsequent sessions usually begin by asking, "What is better?" At first, this may seem somewhat strange, but this question reflects the conviction that solutions are primarily built from the perception of exceptions. Given that both conflict times and exception times will most likely have happened in any client's life since the previous meeting, the opening question might well be the one most useful to the clients, that is, the question about any perceived exceptions that have occurred.

When you ask clients this question, you can expect different responses. Four different groups of clients can be identified on the basis of their responses. The first group is able to identify exceptions that are better since the last meeting. A second group will say, "I don't know. I think things are about the same." A third group will have mixed opinions about the progress they made. One client may say things are better, while the other says things are still the same or worse. The fourth group will say things are worse.

Even within the second, third, and fourth group, with some persistence on the mediator's part, the majority of clients will be able to identify some exceptions. The task of the mediator is to invite clients to talk about all possible details of these exceptions and move in the direction of solutions.

Once an exception is identified, the mediator should explore it in detail. De Jong and Berg (1997) have developed the acronym EARS to capture the mediator's activities in this work. E stands for eliciting the exception. A refers to amplifying it, first by asking the client to describe what is different between this exception time and conflict times and, second, by exploring how the exception happened and especially the role that the client has played in making it happen. R involves reinforcing the successes and strengths the exception represents, largely by noticing exceptions, taking the time to explore them carefully, and complimenting wherever appropriate. Last, S reminds mediators to start again by asking, "What else is better?"

When clients can identify exceptions, whether these exceptions happened in the past or just a short time ago, it is useful to inquire about what it would take for these exceptions to happen again. When clients respond that there is no progress, the mediator may ask a competence question, "How were you able to stabilize the situation?"

When clients do not respond to attempts to explore what is better, and tell you the situation has deteriorated, it is important to respectfully listen to their accounts and accept and normalize their disappointment. This is, however, different from asking details about their failures. After they feel heard, the mediator can move on to ask them competence questions, "How do you manage to keep your heads above water?" or, "How come the situation is not worse than it is?" or, "What has been helpful in the past when there was a setback? Could you perhaps use this strategy again?"

(For a protocol of subsequent meetings, see Appendix 2.)

■ Exercise 9

Start the next ten or twenty seconds of following meetings with the question, "What is better?" Dare to ask that question! You will notice that your clients start anticipating it and, prior to the next meeting, will reflect on what has improved so they can tell you about this.

7 Divorce Mediation

We can gain no lasting peace if we approach it with suspicion and mistrust or with fear. We can gain it only if we proceed with the understanding, the confidence, and the courage which flow from conviction

Franklin D. Roosevelt

Case

Couple C is referred by the Court for arrangements of parental access to their two children, 8 and 10 years old, in the context of a divorce mediation. At the beginning of the meeting, the mediator compliments both ex-partners for the fact that they have shown up and for demonstrating their willingness to investigate how mediation can help them formulate a good arrangement for their children.

They explain that they had seen a mediator earlier, but they were not happy with the process or the outcome. Mrs. C says she signed the agreement too soon because she felt pressure from both her husband and the mediator. Later she discovered that the implementation of the agreement could not be carried out because the details were not sufficiently concrete. The mediator asks, "Given your experience with the previous mediation, what are the dos and don'ts for me in this mediation, to make it a successful one for you?" Mrs. C replies that this time she wants to take it more slowly so better arrangements can be made. The mediator thanks Mrs. C for this tip and asks whether she will concentrate on all the fine details and only agree to a settlement if she really feels comfortable with it and if the implementations are concrete enough and Mrs. C agrees. Then, the mediator asks what issues both want to address in this mediation.

Mrs. C: I will only talk here about the parental access, nothing else.

Mr. C: No, I also want to talk about the maintenance of the children.

Mrs. C: If we are going to talk about the maintenance as well, I would like to discuss other issues, like the money you owe me because I paid for your studies. Then, I would like to discuss what will become our children's principal home, because I might be moving to another city in the future.

Mr. C: I do not want to talk about that here, because then we are going to discuss the previous agreements we made. I don't want that and it is not necessary.

Mrs. C: Then let's just talk about the parental access. For the other things, we may go to court in the future.

Mr. C: No, that doesn't feel good, because I want to talk about maintenance too in this mediation.

Both could not agree what issues should be dealt with. After some time talking back and forth between the couple, the following hypothetical question helped, "Suppose that you could agree on what issues you would discuss here, what issues would you agree on?" Parental access and the distribution of mean were chosen. The mediation could then begin.

The mediator compliments both for their tenacity and their exact wording to speak only about those issues that are important to them. Another compliment is given for the fact that, despite their negative experience with the previous mediator, they decided to mediate their dispute. The mediator remarks that both parents clearly show the motivation to do the best for their children.

Both are asked what their best hopes are. They hope that better mutual cooperation will emerge than is currently the case. This would be particularly beneficial for their children, since they suffer from the tense atmosphere between both parents. Also for the parents themselves, life would be much calmer if a satisfactory arrangement would be agreed upon and both would honor it.

The mediator asks the following scaling question, "How important is it for you, as parents, to have a good collaboration in the interest of your children, where 10 is extremely important and 0 is not important at all?" Both parents indicate that it is very important (Mrs. C says 9, Mr. C says 8.5). After they hear the high mark given by the other, they both appear more willing to work together. The following question is, "Where are you right now on the scale of collaboration, where 10 means you have an optimal collaboration and 0 means you have only conflict?" (Schelling, 1960).

Mrs. C says that she would give it a 2 and Mr. C a 3. The mediatior asks what mark they would like to reach in the future. Mrs. C thinks a 7 would be very good, Mr. C would be satisfied with a 6. The mediator then asks, "What is already working in the right direction?" They note that, in any case, they are again on speaking terms, which had not been the case for a long time. "How did you achieve that?" the mediator asks. It appears that a sister of Mrs. C had played a positive role and had ensured that both meet each other on neutral ground (in a cafe with the sister present) to talk about the children. Also the fact that they decided to see another mediator had been a step in the right direction.

The mediator asks, "What could be the next step?" Mr. C indicates that mutual trust had dropped enormously, owing to recent events. "How could their mutual trust improve?" asks the mediator. Mr. C says he would consider it a sign of trust when Mrs. C would give him her mobile phone number. Given the history of the conflict, Mrs. C is not willing to do so at this time, though she says, "Maybe later." The following question for Mr. C is, "Suppose that Mrs. C were to give you her phone number, what would you do differently?" He says that he would send a birthday card to his daughter (no mediator can make this up!). Mr. C realizes that he can send the card anyway, whether he has the phone number of his ex-partner or not. Later, he decides to do so and, because of this, a small change takes place in the contact between him and the children. This gesture is valued by Mrs. C, and a small positive change takes place between the two ex-partners.

The first meeting ends with the question of whether both think it is necessary or useful to return and if so, when. They both fill in the Session Rating Scale (see Chapter 12 and Appendix 5). As a suggestion for homework, the mediator invites both to take note of moments when they experience a better collaboration and more mutual trust and who does what to make that happen, so at the next meeting they can talk about it.

After three weeks, the second meeting of, again, 90 minutes takes place.

Prior to this meeting, they have a huge argument on the steps of the office of the mediator. The usual opening question, "What is better?" is therefore postponed. When asked where they are on the scale of collaboration, they report that, after the quarrel, they are back to 1 or 0. In the previous weeks, they had gone up to 5 and 6.

The confidence that they can work things out together is now back to zero.

The mediator first acknowledges the disappointment of both and asks, "What would be the smallest thing you could do to make a minimal difference?" Mr. and Mrs. C think long and hard. Subsequently, Mr. C proposes to forget about the quarrel and pretend it did not happen, since the atmosphere in the previous weeks had been much better. Mrs. C initially thinks this is a strange proposal, but then complies. The mediator compliments them with this creative plan.

In this mediation, the future-oriented relationship question that did make a difference was, "Suppose I come across your children in about 10 years time, and I ask them how you collaborated well and managed to settle this conflict in a satisfactory way, what would you like your children to say to me about how you did that?" A long silence followed and tears appeared in Mrs. C's eyes. This question from the perspective of the children made them realize that the mediation was not only about themselves, but mainly about the happiness of their children.

Then the attention is focused on what already worked in the right direction of an adequate collaboration and what steps can take them even further. Also discussed is what they can do themselves, what they need from the other, and how they can even help each other. After the second meeting, both Mr. C and Mrs. C deem further mediation no longer necessary. A written agreement is drafted with clear agreements on the parental access and the distribution of means, the latter consisting of a monthly amount and the payment of additional expenses for both children. The mediator compliments Mrs. C for taking the time to reach this agreement and compliments Mr. C for not wanting to rush things. The mediation is ended. A copy of the written agreement is sent to the Court.

The above case concerns a relationship-focused mediation. It is important in such mediations that the distinction from psychotherapy always remains clear. If the conflict is the focus of attention, and all involved indicate the sessions as mediation, it is indeed mediation. However, if the conversations center on other mutual or personal problems, the mediator will be correct in referring clients to a psychotherapist.

Compliments

Clients have personal qualities and past experiences that, if drawn upon, can be of great use in resolving their difficulties and creating more satisfying lives. These qualities, such as a sense of humor, resilience, and caring for others are the strengths of our clients. Useful past experiences are those in which the client thought about or actually did something that might be put to use in conflict management. These experiences are the client's past successes.

Giving compliments to clients for their qualities and past successes is a powerful tool and is widely used in solution-focused conflict management. Cialdini (1984) states that giving compliments relates to two *weapons of influence*: reciprocation and liking. Giving compliments increases the chances that the other person will be nicer too, because people who provide praise are liked better and because the rule of reciprocation will oblige the other person to do so. Cialdini cites a study done on men in North Carolina. The men in the study received comments about themselves from another person who needed a favor from them. Some of the men got only positive comments, some got only negative comments, and some got a mixture of both. There were three interesting findings. First, the men liked the evaluator who provided only praise best. Second, this was the case even though the men fully realized that the man who provided praise stood to gain from their liking him. Finally, unlike the other types of comments, pure praise did not have to be accurate to work. Positive comments produced just as many good feelings for the person who provided praise when they were untrue as when they were true.

Arts et al. (1994) found that systematic use of compliments in psychotherapy not only ensures a positive alliance between therapist and clients, but also enhances the outcome of psychotherapy no less than 30%, compared to psychotherapy in which compliments are not given.

There are different type of compliments. A *direct compliment* is a positive evaluation or reaction by the mediator in response to the client. It can be about something the client has said, done, or made or about his appearance. A compliment can also be about the client's strengths or resources, "You must be a real caring mother to.........tell me more about that." or, "You must be a very determined person, please tell me more about this determination of yours."

An *indirect compliment* is a question that implies something positive about the client. One way to indirectly compliment is to ask for more information about a desired outcome stated by the client. These questions invite the client to tell a success story, "How did you do this? How were you able to ......? Where did you get this wonderful idea?"

In giving compliments to several people it is very important to pay attention to an equal share of the compliments. Compliments can be given to each person individually or to the persons together, "Apparently you all succeed in the past to work together in a pleasant way. Could you tell me how you did that back then?"

Indirect complimenting is preferable to direct complimenting because its questioning format leads clients to discover and state their own strengths and resources.

Many clients accept compliments easily. Others downplay or even reject them. But remember that the first goal in giving compliments is for clients to notice their positive changes, strengths, and resources. It is not necessary for them to openly accept the compliments.

■ Exercise 10

In the next conversations that lasts longer than five minutes, give at least three compliments to those present and notice how the atmosphere of the conversations changes.

Story 7: The Importance of Accepting Compliments

One day a pretty young snake bathed by the edge of a lake. Having washed, she stretched out on a warm rock to dry, and began to preen herself. A fly buzzing by looked down, saw her, and commented: 'My, your scales are gleaming so attractively in the sunlight. You look sleek and clean. You are such a beautiful snake!'

The snake, shy and embarrassed, slithered off to hide. Seeing a hut nearby, she disappeared through the thatched grass walls. She did not realize it was the home of the village sorcerer. Frightened, he grabbed his drum and started beating it loudly to frighten away this evil intruder.

A tortoise who was slowly journeying across an adjoining field heard the rhythmic beat of the drum and began to dance. An elephant, seeing this unseemly display from such a sedate creature, stood on the tortoise's back. The tortoise excreted fire, and the fire ignited the sorcerer's tinder-dry grass hut. Black clouds billowed up into the sky, darkening the land. A deluge of rain fell from the heavens but quickly abated, allowing the sun to spread its warm and drying light. A mother ant, seizing the opportunity to dry her eggs following the flood of rain, spread them in the sun. An anteater, quick to see an opportunity for a meal, gobbled down the ant's eggs.

The ant took the anteater to court. Seeking redress under the laws of the land, she approached the judge of the jungle, the king of beasts, and described her problem. The lion convened a court, calling together all the parties involved. First he addressed the anteater. 'Anteater, why did you eat the ant's eggs?'

'Well', the anteater replied, 'I am an anteater. That is my role or destiny. I was only doing what came naturally. What other alternative was there for me when the ant spread her eggs so temptingly in front of me?' Turning to the ant, the lion asked: 'Ant, why did you spread your eggs where they might tempt the anteater?' 'It was not my intent to tempt the anteater. Surely you an see I am a better mother than that but what else could I do to care for my young?' replied the ant. 'They got wet in the heavy deluge of rain. They needed to dry out and the sun shone so warmly.'

Looking to the sun, the lion continued his investigation. 'Sun, why did you shine?' 'What else could I do?' asked the sun. 'It is my job. The rain had poured and, as everyone knows, the sun must follow the rain.' 'Rain, why did you pour?' asked the lion in his search to unravel the truth. 'What else could I do?' responded the rain. 'The sorcerer's hut was on fire, the whole village was under threat, I only wanted to help.'

'Hut, why did you catch on fire?' 'I could not do anything else once the tortoise excreted fire on me', answered the charred remnants of the sorcerer's hut. 'I was made of grass. I had stood there for years. I was very dry and had no resistance.'

'Tortoise', inquired the king of beasts, 'why did you excrete fire?' 'It was the only thing I could do. The elephant stood on me. With her weight, my life was threatened. I had to do something to try to escape.'

The lion looked up at the elephant. 'Tell me, why did you tread on the tortoise?' "What else was there to do?' asked the elephant. 'She danced so wildly. Her behavior was most unbecoming and inappropriate for a tortoise. I thought she had gone crazy or something. I didn't intend to hurt her. I just wanted to help settle her wild mood.'

The lion turned back to the tortoise. "Why was it you were dancing so wildly?'
'What else could I do, responded the tortoise. 'The sorcerer was beating out such rhythmic and compelling dance music on his drum, I had no choice, I just had to dance.' 'Sorcerer, why were you beating your drum?' The sorcerer answered: 'What else was there for me to do when the snake entered my hut? She frightened me. She was dangerous. Serpents are the representations of evil forces and bad omens. I had to chase its evil presence out of my home.'

'Snake', inquired the king of beasts, patiently working his way through the line of witnesses, 'why did you enter the sorcerer's hut?' 'What else could I do?, answered the snake. 'The fly embarrassed me with its words of praise. Somehow, somewhere I had to hide my face, and the grass hut of the sorcerer was the closest refuge.'

Finally the lion turned to the fly. 'Fly, why did you praise the snake?'
The fly did not address the king of beasts but instead turned to look at the snake and asked: 'What? Don't you know how to take a compliment?'

8 Working Alliance and Motivation to Change

If you want to build a ship,
Don't drum up people to collect wood and
Don't assign them tasks and work,
But rather teach them to long for the endless immensity of the sea
Antoine de Saint-Exupéry

Motivation to Change

It would be nice if both clients and mediator could begin with the assumption that the mediation procedure is being used as intended: to find solutions together, to re-establish dialogue, to settle a case, or to put something behind them. For this, sometimes changes in personal behavior are required. However, commitment to mediation and the motivation to make these personal behavior changes are not synonymous. If a client is willing to participate in mediation (commitment) this does not necessarily signify that he is also willing to change his own behavior. Often clients will (silently) hope that the mediator will see the other person as the one who is to blame for the conflict so that only his behavior needs to change.

In a solution-focused approach, which is described in much more detail by Bannink (2008f), it is the task and challenge of the mediator to assist clients in making changes and to help them leave the ditches they have dug themselves into.

This chapter discusses the methods of assessing the clients' motivation to change and how this change can be encouraged, so that a positive outcome in mediation is enhanced. In this process, the mediator assesses the type of relationship he has with each client to optimize cooperation.

Visitor, Complainant, or Customer

The mediator assesses in the first meeting his working relationship with each client: Does it concern a visitor, a complainant, or a customer relationship? For convenience, the terms are shortened to *visitor, complainant,* and *customer,* although they do not refer to a quality of the client as such, but always to the type of relationship between the mediator and each individual client. The challenge for the mediator is to invite each client to become (or remain) a customer. It often happens that clients will start mediation from a visitor or a complainant relationship. This early assessment of each client's level of motivation is of essential importance for the strategy of the mediator and for any homework suggestions.

In a visitor relationship, the client is mandated (by court, insurance company, employer). This involuntary client has no conflict personally, others have a conflict with him. Naturally, he is not motivated to change his behavior. Often the mandated client's goal is to maintain the relationship with the person referring him or to free himself from this person as soon as possible.

The mediator creates a climate in which a call for help is made possible. What does the client want to achieve through his relationship with the mediator? What would the person referring him like to see changed in his behavior as a result of the mediation and to what extent is the client prepared to cooperate in this? Some tips:

- Assume that the client has good reasons for thinking and behaving as they do.
- Do not be judgmental, and inquire into the perceptions of the client that make their – often defensive – attitude understandable.
- Ask what the client thinks the person referring them would like to see changed at the end of the mediation.
- Ask the client their opinion on this and what their minimum input might be.

In a complainant-relationship, the client has a conflict and is suffering from it, but does not see their part of the conflict and/or the solutions. The Client does not feel the need to change their own behavior but thinks the other, or something else, is to blame for the conflict and should change.

The mediator gives acknowledgment and asks about competencies (for example, "How do you manage?"). The mediator invites the client to talk about exceptions, moments when the conflict is or was there to a lesser extent, or about the moments when there is already a sign or small part of what the client does want instead of what he does not want. Thus, the client is invited to think and talk about his preferred future (without the conflict) rather than focusing on the conflict. Walter and Peller (1992) describe four strategies that may be applied in a complainant relationship:

- "I wish I could help you with this, but I am not a magician. I do not think that anyone is able to change anyone else. How else might I help you?" or "In what way is this conflict a problem for you?"
- Investigating the hypothetical solution, "Imagine the other changing in the direction desired, what would you notice different about them? What would you notice different about yourself? What difference would that make to your relationship with them? At what moments is this already occurring?"

- Investigating the future if the other is not changing, "What can you still do yourself?"
- Figuring out the hoped for outcome behind earlier attempts, "What do you finally hope to achieve together?"

Case

Neighbor A, living on the first floor, experiences noise nuisance from neighbor B on the ground floor. Late at night, friends visit neighbor B and they drink and shout a lot.

Neighbor A has called the police many times, but they have not done much. Neighbor B, an alcoholic, does not think there is any problem. When both present themselves for mediation, referred by their housing association, neighbor A can be characterized as a *complainant* (neighbor B needs to change) and neighbor B as a *visitor* (I have no problem or conflict).

In a customer relationship, the client is also suffering from the conflict, does see themself as part of the conflict and/or the solution, and is motivated to change their behavior. In the request for help the word "I" or "we" is present, "What can I do to solve this conflict?" or, "How can we ensure that we re-establish a good relationship or split in the best possible way?" Mediation with two "customers" is often the "icing on the cake."

In the first meeting, it is common to find that both clients are complainants and think that the other needs to change. The trichotomy between visitor, complainant, and customer is a value-free continuum: Each position of the client is validated and accepted. The fact that the client has shown up at all makes them already a visitor, because they could also have chosen not to attend. Cialdini (1984) states that the rule for reciprocation ("much obliged") and liking the other person (the mediator) are strong weapons of influence. Giving compliments to the clients helps in establishing a good relationship.

One of the principles of *motivational interviewing* (Miller & Rollnick, 2002) is unconditional acceptance of the client's position. The professional builds a relationship that is based on collaboration, individual responsibility, and autonomy. Miller and Rollnick state that the necessity of approaching the client in a nonmoralizing way is impeded if the professional is unprepared or unable to defer their own (mistaken) ideas about problem behavior and labels the client's behavior.

The professional reacts with empathy, avoids discussions, and strengthens the clients' self-efficacy. Miller and Rollnick describe the (solution-focused) term *change talk*. This is a method of communication used for enhancing the client's intrinsic motivation to change by stressing the advantages of the behavior change. This change talk assists the client in preparing for change. As methods for professionals to elicit change talk, they mention asking open-ended questions, such as, "How would you like to see things change? How would you want your life to look in five years time?" By inviting clients to talk about their preferred future (their goal), their competencies and successes, and to look for the exceptions, moments that were or are successful, the mediator will encourage visitors and complainants to transform into customers. Asking competence questions stimulates clients to talk about successes and to give self-compliments, which feeds their feeling of self-worth. Bannink (2007a, b) states that focusing on the preferred future facilitates change in the desired direction. Therefore, focus on what you do want instead of what you don't want.

■ Exercise 11

Choose a partner for this exercise. Ask your partner to complain about a third person that he would like to change. Ask your partner to talk about the same complaint every time, so you can practice with the four different strategies described in this chapter. Notice the differences brought about by each strategy. Then, change roles. In the role of the client, you can learn a lot from the different types of questions that are asked of you.

Attitude of the Solution-Focused Mediator

In solution-focused conflict management, the attitude of the mediator is different from the attitude of the traditional mediator. The solution-focused attitude can be described as *not-knowing* and *leading from one step behind.*

Solution-focused mediators work in ways that allow clients to be the experts about their own experiences and what these mean. They think the best way to lead clients is the solution-focused way of leading from one step behind. They adopt a posture of not-knowing and develop interviewing skills that allow clients to provide information about themselves and their situation. They do not pull or push, they are not leading. Clients are considered to be the experts of their own lives and the mediator asks solution-focused questions to invite clients to inform the mediator and to come up with their own solutions to the conflict. This attitude promotes client trust, confidence, and hopefulness about the future.

Resistance Is Not a Useful Concept

De Shazer (1984) proposes that what professionals see as signs of resistance are, in fact, the unique ways in which clients choose to cooperate. For example, clients who do not carry out the assigned homework, do not demonstrate resistance, but are actually cooperating because in that way they are indicating that this homework is not in accordance with their way of doing things. De Shazer assumes that clients are competent in figuring out what they want, and in which way they can achieve this. It is the mediator's task to assist clients in discovering these competencies and using them to create their preferred future.

With resistance as a central concept, therapist and client are like opposing tennis players. They are engaged in fighting against each other, and the therapist needs to win in order for the therapy to succeed. With cooperation as a central concept, therapist and client are like tennis players on the same side of the net. Cooperating is a necessity, although sometimes it becomes necessary to fight alongside your partner so that you can cooperatively defeat your mutual opponent' (p. 13).

In this case, the opponent is the conflict. This view relates to the narrative approach (Winslade & Monk, 2000), in which externalizing the conflict, turning the conflict into the enemy, is a much-used intervention. In Erickson's view, resistance is cooperative; it is one of the possible responses people can make to interventions.

If the mediator feels that he is becoming irritated, insecure, or demoralized, *countertransference* is taking place. That is, the negative reaction of the mediator to the behavior of the client. This may happen when the mediator, wrongly, considers the client a customer when the individual is still a visitor or a complainant.

When clients are angry or seem to be unmotivated with regard to a particular topic, it is useful for the mediator to remind themself that clients are competent and that it is important to look for a way to cooperate with them. Then, resistance becomes a signal that the mediator needs to formulate a question about what the resistance suggests is important to the client, instead of concluding that the client is resistant or unmotivated. This applies equally to voluntary and involuntary clients.

Case

In a neighbor mediation, the mediator gives the clients a homework assignment, "Between now and the next time we meet, I would like you to observe, so you can describe to me the next time we meet, what happens in your relationship that you want to continue to have happen."

This intervention is an attempt to define mediation as dealing with the present and the future, rather than the past. The mediator expects something worthwhile to happen and this is opposite of what the neighbors expect to happen. From this perspective, the assignment lets the neighbors know that the mediator expects change and is confident that change will occur. This assignment is an easy task for the neighbors to cooperate on, since it does not call for anything different. Only observations are required. This is something the neighbors will do anyway, and the assignment simply attempts to direct the focus of their observations.

Scaling Motivation, Confidence, and Hope

Question: How many mediators does it take to change a lightbulb?
Answer: One, but the lightbulb has really got to want to change

Scaling questions about motivation, confidence, and hope to change can be used to find out how motivated, confident, and hopeful clients are that the mediation will be successful. Asking competence questions (How were you able to do that? How did you decided to do that?) also helps to increase motivation, confidence, and hope. Moreover, scaling questions are equally valid for the mediator, who can assess their own motivation, confidence, and hope. Questions for scaling motivation are:
- "If 10 means that you will do anything to reach your hoped for outcome. and 0 means that you will just wait and see, at what point on the scale are you right now?"
- When your client gives a high score, for example a 7 or 8, you may ask, "Where does this willingness to work hard come from?"
- When your client give a low score, for example a 2, you may ask, "How did you manage to reach a 2, how come it is not a 0 or 1?" The follow-up question could be, "What would a 3 look like?" and, "What is required to move up one point on the motivation scale?"
- "Suppose you gave your motivation a higher score, what would you notice different about yourself? What would be different in your relationship with the other person?"

The mediator can also ask how confident or hopeful clients are that they will reach their preferred future:
- If 10 means that you are completely confident that you will reach your hoped for outcome and 0 means that you have no confidence at all, "Where on the scale would you say you are right now?"
- When your client gives a high score, you may ask, "You seem to be the type of person that, once a decision to tackle something has been made,

has a strong belief that you will succeed." or, "Where does this high level of confidence (or hope) come from?"

- When your client gives a low score, for example a 3, you may ask, "How did you manage to reach a 3 despite the situation? What would one point up look like? What is needed to move up one point on the scale? What can you do yourself and what do you need from the other person?"
- "Suppose you would give your confidence (or hope) a higher score, what would you notice different about yourself? What would be different in your relationship with the other person?"

Thomas-Kilmann Conflict Mode Instrument

Kilmann and Thomas (1977) developed a conflict style inventory that identifies five major ways that people approach conflict and negotiation. They also developed an instrument to measure an individual's preferred mode. In practice, very few people will conform consistently to a single mode, but it is important to remain cognizant of these five modes whenever we are negotiating. The model helps to identify an individual's preferred method for dealing with conflict, it helps people understand how others try to resolve conflict, and it teaches skills to identify more appropriate methods of conflict resolution. It can be useful for both individuals and groups.

There are two dimensions in the model: from assertive to passive, and from uncooperative to cooperative. Within these dimensions, people can vary from competing (assertive/uncooperative) to avoiding (passive/uncooperative), and from collaborating (assertive/cooperative) to accommodating (passive/cooperative).

Negotiators and mediators need to be aware of people that may slip into the avoidance or accommodation modes when they need to be present and at the table – alternatively, people that are too quick to leap into an aggressive competitive mode need to be encouraged into more cooperative modes to resolve their conflict.

The collaborating mode is generally preferred, and is the mode most likely to result in a win-win outcome. Expert mediators should be able to use all five modes. Each of the five basic modes has advantages and disadvantages depending on context. These five basic modes are comparable with the working relationship between mediator and client: the visitor, complainant, and customer relationship (see earlier in this Chapter).

Persuasion Theory

Much has been written on the psychology of persuasion and influence. What techniques and strategies are most commonly and effectively used by a broad range of compliance practitioners, from car salesmen to doctors and lawyers? Cialdini (1984) states that although there are thousands of different tactics that compliance practitioners employ to produce "yes," the majority fall within six basis categories, each one governed by a fundamental psychological principle that directs human behavior, and, in doing so, gives the tactics their power. These categories are: consistency, reciprocation, social proof, authority, liking, and scarcity.

In contrast to the one-time and unidirectional message transmissions that characterize persuasion when someone is buying a car, conflicts involve dynamic and repeated interactions between people who are simultaneously senders and recipients of persuasive messages. Clients in mediation engage in bidirectional, mutual-influence attempts at persuasion. These attempts may also be directed not only at one's opponent, but also at the mediator and the lawyers involved. In negotiations and mediation, the source and the target of attempts at influence are interdependent: Their outcomes depend on one another's actions. If clients were autonomous, decisions could be made independently without interaction, and negotiations or mediation would not be necessary.

Persuasion typically involves influence to change beliefs, in addition to eliciting behavioral compliance. Persuasion involves changing another person's mind about what is in their best interest in the context of a particular conflict. If persuasion is successful, then the old beliefs and attitudes are changed and new ones internalized, so that the behavioral change that ensues is, in fact, consistent with one's beliefs and attitudes.

Settlements will often fall apart if the participants to the settlement do not truly belief that it is in their self-interest. For a settlement to stand the test of time, all participants have to be persuaded that the settlement is in some sense optimal. Successful conflict resolution (in the sense of arriving at a mutually agreeable solution) necessarily must involve social influence that goes beyond attempts at coercion and relies on persuasion. Coercion involves attempts to influence another person to behave in a certain way (and maybe accept a suboptimal resolution) and is therefore not desirable.

Persuasion is an opportunity for clients to increase the breadth and depth of their knowledge about the conflict and, from a solution-focused point of view, especially what they would like to have instead of the conflict. This can be helpful in identifying integrative outcomes. It can also lead to cognitive changes that will increase internalization of agreement and, hence, the probability that agreements are stable across time and situation.

Kevin Hogan, an expert on influence, describes on his website www.kevinhogan.com, how looking to the future facilitates change in the desired direction:

> A new scientific breakthrough in gaining compliance allows you to bring your communication partner out into the future and imagine what it might be like to buy your product or service. Regardless of whether this is a positive or negative thought process, the customer is more likely to buy from you (or say yes to a date), just for having gone out into the future to imagine the buying process or the dating process.

Caucus

If clients no longer wish to participate in a meeting, the clients that stay may still be invited to work on the relationship. If a part of the system changes, the whole system changes. Relationship questions can be used to bring the missing person into the room, "Suppose the other was here, what do you think they would say they want to see different, knowing them as well as you do?"

In solution-focused conflict management, the use of caucus – separate conversations with the clients – is used as little as possible. If clients themselves want to have an individual conversation with the mediator, the mediator will ask, "How do you think this conversation might be useful?" If there are separate (intake) interviews, as in a consulting hour for neighbors, where one of the neighbors (or more) complains about another neighbor, solution-focused questions can be used. For example, questions about the goal of the mediation can be asked. After the other neighbor(s) has told his story, they can repeat their hopes in the first joint meeting.

An argument against the use of caucus may also be that the oxytocin level (see Chapter 11) cannot rise if clients don't meet each other at the mediator's table. Even a handshake at the beginning and/or end of the mediation increases the oxytocin level. In the animal kingdom, holding hands, stroking, or grooming often accompanies reconciliation.

Working Alliance

Clinical researchers have been focussing on the one aspect of psychotherapy that seems to make little difference, i.e., the type of therapy delivered. Psychologist contributions to outcomes overwhelm treatment differences: The person of the psychologist is critical. The most researched common factor – the *alliance* between the psychologist and the patient – has been found to be a robust predictor of outcome, even when measured early in therapy (Wampold, 2001). Regardless of theoretical orientation or professional discipline, the strength of the relationship between the professional and the client is consistently associated with effective treatment outcome. This is true, in particular, for the client's assessment of the relationship, not the professional's assessment. Their ratings of the alliance have a stronger correlation with outcome than the ratings of professionals. Moreover, ratings at early stages of treatment are more predictive of outcome than ratings taken later in the process.

Nevertheless, only a few psychotherapy studies have been designed to assess psychological effects, despite the fact that ignoring them biases the results. The evidence-based treatment movement places emphasis on treatments when it has been found that the type of treatment accounts for very little of the variability in outcomes. Aspects of treatment that are valued by psychologists and patients and that have been shown to account for variability in outcomes have been ignored.

Research shows that alliance is particularly predictive of outcome when measured early in treatment; poor early alliance predicts client dropout. The implication is that attention must be paid to the alliance as soon as mediation begins, because these findings concerning the alliance in psychotherapy will probably be the same for the alliance in mediation. Keijsers, Schaap, and Hoogduin (2000) also found that there are two clusters of therapist behaviors that are associated with a positive outcome: (a) the conditions of empathy, nonpossessive warmth, positive regard, and genuineness and (b) the therapeutic alliance.

"Supermediators"

It is obvious that not every mediator is equally successful. Wampold (2001) notes that, as some lawyers have better results, some artists create more remarkable works of art, and students perform better with some teachers than others, some psychotherapists also will achieve better results than others. Therefore, most of us, when we recommend a mediator, lawyer, doctor, or psychotherapist to a friend or relative, we rely more on the competence and expertise of this person than on his theoretical background.

Miller et al. (1997) found that recent studies show solid empirical evidence for what distinguishes highly effective therapists ('Supershrinks') from other therapists. The data show that clients of the best clinicians achieve 50% or more improvement and 50% or fewer dropouts than those seen by average practitioners. Surprisingly, training, certification, supervision, years of experience, and even use of evidence-based practices do not contribute to superior performance. Research conducted over the last 30 years documents that the effectiveness rates of most clinicians plateaus very early in training, despite the fact that most professionals believe they improve with time and experience.

Despite the important role played by the mediator or psychotherapist, it is clear from the research that our knowledge exhibits major gaps. We still know surprisingly little about the variables and qualities that are the characteristics of a competent and effective *supertherapist* or *supermediator* and about the interaction of these variables with different approaches in therapy or mediation. We know even less about the interaction with clients or client variables.

Wampold (2001) gives an overview of research in psychotherapy. One chapter in his book is about *allegiance*: the faith the professional has in his own treatment model. The faith one has in the treatment and the capacity of that treatment to help clients change, is an important quality of a competent professional. When the professional does not invest sufficiently in his treatment, this may endanger the treatment outcome. Allegiance toward a treatment is based on the idea that if a professional is favorably disposed toward a treatment and experiences the positive effects of that treatment, he will execute this treatment with more perseverance, enthusiasm, hope, and competence.

Research on the impact of variables of therapist characteristics shows that competent, creative, committed therapists can often smooth out any restriction on their age, gender, or color of skin (Beutler et al., 2004). There is a consistent relationship between a positive and friendly attitude of the therapist and a positive outcome. A critical and hostile attitude has the opposite effect. A *supertherapist* or *supermediator* seeks, obtains, and maintains more consumer engagement. Another consistent outcome of research is that it is important that therapists are sufficiently active and directive to ensure that their clients do not simply repeat their dysfunctional patterns and that they structure the sessions sufficiently to stimulate clients to face up to their cognitions and behavior.

Miller et al. (1997) show that good professionals are much more likely to ask for and receive negative feedback about the quality of the work and their contribution to the alliance. The best clinicians, those falling in the top 25% of treatment outcomes, consistently achieve lower scores on standardized alliance measures *at the outset* of therapy – perhaps because they are more persistent or are more believable when assuring clients that they want honest answers – enabling them to address potential problems in the working relationship. Median therapists, by contrast, commonly receive negative feedback later in treatment, at a time when clients have already disengaged and are at heightened risk for dropping out. So supertherapists or supermediators are exceptionally alert to the risk of dropping out and treatment failure.

Most aspects of the style of the therapist are strongly dependent on whether the therapist adjusts to the preferences, hopes, and characteristics of his clients. He should give fewer directives if the client does not comply and he should adjust his style to hold a moderate arousal (not too much and not too little), because a moderate arousal promotes change. Flexibility and building rapport are, therefore, essential qualities for a therapist. The specific responses from the therapist that are responsible for a positive working alliance vary from client to client. Good therapists are sensitive to the reactions of their clients and can adjust their interactions on the basis of this feedback (Duncan, Miller & Sparks, 2004).

Norcross (2002) and Wampold and Bhati (2004) found that the personality of the professional and the alliance with their client are far more powerful determinants of the outcome of the meetings than the choice of methodology. The therapist's degree of comfort with closeness in interpersonal relationships, low hostility, and high social support predicted client's ratings of the alliance early in treatment. Additionally, they found that therapist experience was not predictive of the strength of any aspect of the therapeutic relationship.

In sum, the therapist is in many ways intertwined with change. In most models of change the therapist is central and it depends on the therapist whether and how change mechanisms operate in the therapeutic process. The expectation is that this research into the role of the therapist also applies to other professionals such as doctors, lawyers, and mediators (Bannink, 2009a, 2009b).

■ Exercise 12

Make your own *Certificate of Competence* (see John Wheeler's website – Certificate of Competence: A self-coaching tool for optimising professional practice, http://www.johnwheeler.co.uk/resources/certificate_of_competence.php). This certificate is a self-coaching tool for optimising professional practice. Ask yourself these seven questions:

- When I do my work, I take my inspiration from the following people:
- These people have taught me that when I do my work it is most important to remember the following:
- These are the people who encourage me to do the work I do:
- They encouraged me to do this work because they noticed the following about me:
- When I do my work, the people I deal with are likely to appreciate that I have the following qualities and abilities:
- These are the people in my support network who know I have these qualities and abilities:
- If I am under pressure at work and can only remember one quality or ability it should be this:

Motivation of the Mediator

The mediator also needs to be motivated to help clients reach their preferred future. The responsibility for a good alliance not only rests with the clients but equally with the mediator. If no progress is being made, the mediator can ask himself these questions:

- If I asked the clients how my contribution has helped so far, even though it may only be a little bit, how would they respond?
- What do the clients see as a sign(s) of a successful result?
- How realistic is this result?
- What do I see as a sign(s) of success?
- If my ideas and those of my clients differ, what needs to be done for me to work toward their goal?
- Where on the scale of 10 to 0 would the clients say that they are right now?
- What should happen for them to be able to achieve a score closer to 10?
- How much motivation, hope, or confidence do I have as a mediator that this mediation will be successful? Suppose I would have more motivation, hope, or confidence, what would I then be doing differently? And what difference would that make to my clients?

If the mediator is no longer motivated, confident, or hopeful (see above) that they can help clients reach their preferred future, they should examine what needs to be done to regain motivation, confidence, or hope themself. When the mediator has a complainant relationship (they may be irritated or discouraged) and is no longer motivated to re-establish a positive cooperation with clients, it is advisable that they re-assign the mediation to a colleague.

■ Exercise 13

Which clients in your caseload might be involuntary clients? Which ones of your clients indicated that they wanted something out of the mediation? Does the client want to achieve something himself (then he is a *customer)*? Does he want somebody else to change, then he is a *complainant.* Or are there others involved who want something from this client? In that case, your client can be regarded as a visitor.

Remember, everyone sitting at the mediator's table has a goal. What might be the goal of the mandated client at your table?

9 Neighbor Conflict Mediation

One day we must come to see that peace is not merely a distant goal we seek, but that it is a means by which we arrive at that goal. We must pursue peaceful ends through peaceful means
Martin Luther King

Case

Neighbor A, living on the first floor, experiences noise nuisance from neighbor B on the second floor. Late at night he habitually plays his guitar and walks on the laminate floor. This keeps neighbor A and his wife awake so this has increasingly annoyed him. He has knocked on the door of neighbor B many times to ask if it is possible to keep the noise down. Neighbor B, however, thinks that he has the right to make music in his own home and according to him walking on the laminate floor does not make a noise. When both present themselves for mediation, referred by their housing association, neighbor A can be characterized as a complainant (the other needs to change) and neighbor B as a visitor (he is mandated: I have no conflict).

After the first preliminary arrangements and building some rapport by asking about the neighbors' lives and hobbies, the mediator compliments both, "I am impressed that you came, it is not something most people enjoy doing! Especially since the housing association ordered you in for mediation!" Both neighbors look a bit uneasy. Then, they are both given one opportunity to say "what definitely has to be said."

Both neighbors take this opportunity to explain the conflict, to which the mediator listens carefully and respectfully. The mediator does not probe for further details about the conflict. However, there is acknowledgment of the impact of the conflict on the lives of both of them and their environment. The mediator states that it surely must be difficult to live in the same building with everything that is going on at this moment.

Then the mediator asks the question about their best hopes. Initially, both remain silent, then neighbor B says that he has no hopes whatsoever. He has been mandated by the housing association; he does not think this mediation will be helpful at all. This will certainly be the only time he will be sitting at the table of the mediator.

The mediator acknowledges that neighbor B is an involuntary client and has not come out of free will. Since they are here anyway, maybe they could all find out together what the housing association would like to see happen by the end of the mediation? And maybe then neighbor B could consider to what extent he would be prepared to comply with this? Neighbor A has his own agenda; he would like to see the mediator put him in the right and declare neighbor B in the wrong.

The mediator tries to normalize the conflict to some extent: noise nuisance is very common in the old apartments where both live; so many people have conflicts about it. Both say they indeed heard such stories. The miracle question is put forward, "Suppose a miracle happened tonight, and the conflict that brought you here were to be solved. But you did not know, because you were both asleep. What would be the first sign tomorrow morning that would tell you that things have changed?" Both neighbors then give exactly the same answer, "I would wake up, look out of the window, and see a huge removal truck. I am not moving, he is!" The mediator asks what difference that would make. Also here they say the same thing: There would be peace and quiet and they would not have to see each other ever again.

The mediator says that this would be a very good outcome for all, if only this would come true! Neither would have to spend their energy on the conflict anymore. "How real do you think this beautiful scenario is?" asks the mediator. They both laugh a bit, because they are clearly not prepared to be the moving one. Then, they are asked if they are willing to look for alternatives, given the fact that they apparently both want to stay in the same place and since the housing association wants them to find solutions together. After some hesitation they agree.

What has already been working in the right direction? What have they tried so far and what has helped, even just a little bit? Neighbor B says he has a small house outside the city where he goes sometimes in the weekends to play music and his guitar. On those weekends, all is quiet for neighbor A. Neighbor A has put his bed in another room of the house, so he and his wife are less affected by the noise at night. He also wears earplugs, although he would prefer to sleep without them. His wife tries to calm him down sometimes when he gets irritated.

The mediator compliments both on finding workable solutions. What would be the next step or next sign of progress? What could neighbor A and B do themselves? And what do they need from each other? And what do they think the housing association wants to see different? They think the housing association wants them to behave as reasonable tenants who leave each other alone.

At the end of the first meeting of 2 hours, the mediator gives feedback to the clients. Compliments are given, "I think it is a good thing that you decided not to make the conflict worse than it is today. I am impressed with what you have already achieved so far, although I understand that this is not enough. I am also impressed with what you have done to prevent the conflict from getting worse than it actually is. You explained earlier in this meeting that you try to avoid meeting each other as much as possible, so the conflict will not escalate."

Would they both be willing to come again one time? The answer is affirmative. A suggestion is given to think about the possible next small steps they are prepared to take, so they can talk about those the next meeting. The Session Rating Scale is also used; they are both satisfied with the first meeting (above 30, see Chapter 12).

After two weeks, the neighbors are back at the table. "What is better?" asks the mediator. Neighbor A smiles and says, "Everything!" He explains that neighbor B has been on a holiday, so they could enjoy peace and quiet in the house. That must have felt great, the mediator comments.

Both have been thinking about the next small steps. Neighbor A says he is thinking of asking the housing association to help him to make the ceiling of his apartment soundproof, and how he could share the costs. Neighbor B has put a carpet on the floor of the living room, so the sound of the footsteps has become less. He is thinking of leaving the city now every weekend. He will take his guitar, so he can play without someone becoming irritated.

The mediator compliments both on their steps in the right direction. It is clear that they are both working hard to find peace again. What would be their hoped for outcome now? They say they want to leave each other in peace. Neighbor A says, "And maybe even greet each other on the stairs again." When asked, he says he will take the leading role in this: The next time they meet on the stairs, he will be the first to greet the other. He hopes neighbor B will then greet back. Neighbor B says he will think about that. The mediator compliments both on these positive steps. Do they want another meeting? They don't think so, they say. A written agreement is not necessary for them. The mediator ends the mediation. In three months time the mediator contacts them and asks again, "What is better?" The relationship has improved somewhat further and the housing association is pleased with the result.

Normalization

De Jong and Berg (1997) state:

Clients who are struggling with emotionally charged difficulties often lose perspective. Unable to find satisfactory solutions and caught up in the pain and tension of the moment, they come to think and talk as though their problems are out of control and beyond the bounds of normalcy (p. 42).

Professionals can easily get caught up in this intense problem talk and lose their capacity to formulate solution-building questions.

Normalizing involves responding to problem talk by wondering with clients about whether their difficulties are not within the range of ordinary problems of living. Normalizing must be done naturally and confidently or clients may feel the mediator is minimizing their struggles. It is useful in solution building because it offers clients a chance to normalize their conflict, and it helps both clients and professionals to clarify what clients want different.

Normalization of setbacks is also important, since many clients regard problems and solutions in all or none terms. The first time there is a setback, clients easily think that the change does not count or that the changing is not real. While changing, clients are often vulnerable to thoughts of failure. A more positive approach introduces the notion that change usually involves some setbacks. For every three steps forward, there are one or two steps back. After this type of normalization, clients are invited to notice how they get themselves back on track when the setback occurs.

Story 8: Drawing Boundaries

Once there were two countries. Over the years, and as a result of many struggles, they had drawn a boundary that defined the extent of their lands. As one country was very strong, and the other did not have stones, they simply followed the geological line of where the stones began and ended. At first all was well, then the people on the stony side began to envy those on the stoneless side, thinking if their own land was clear, they could till the soil, grow crops and feed their people without having to move rock after rock. The people on the stoneless side envied those with the stones, thinking how stones would be useful to build houses and construct fences. Each wanted what the other had, and did not appreciate what they already possessed. The people on the stony land went to their queen and complained about all the stones. Eventually she relented to their demands and said 'OK, if you don't want the stones, throw them across the border.' The people of the stoneless country went to their king and complained 'The people in the queen's country are throwing stones at us.' The king said 'How dare they invade our territory. This is an act of war.'

The war continued for some time with stones being hurled back and forth across the border until the king had a bright idea. He said to his military chiefs 'Don't we want stones? Let's keep wagging war with the queen's people. For they are poor and have no other weapons apart from their stones. That way we will have all the material we need to construct our buildings.' So the war continued until the stoneless land was full of stones and the stony land had no stones.

Again, for a while, both the king's and queen's subjects were happy. The queen's people tilled the lands and produced crops. The king's people built homes and stone fences. Then discontentment arose again. The queen's subjects had no materials to build new homes and the king's subjects had so little clear land that they couldn't grow crops.

The countries declared war once more and hurled the stones back across the border at each other. And so the cycle of conflict continued, broken only by brief periods of peace when the two countries were busy growing crops or erecting new buildings. But neither king nor queen was happy, and each began to think how much nicer it would be if their countries could live in harmony instead of conflict. Musing with the idea of what it would be like to talk instead of fight, they arranged to meet in a neutral country, where, for a while, they could distance themselves from their history of conflict. The talks weren't easy at first, for there had been many years of bitterness. 'It is all your fault' said the king. 'You started this by throwing stones at us.' The queen replied 'Maybe there are accusations I can make about you too. There have been many bad feelings between our countries, but it will not help us to find a resolution if we fall into the trap of blaming each other.'

The king acknowledged that to reach a solution they would have to put aside the feelings of anger, hostility, and bitterness that had built up in the past. 'What has been is something we can't alter' said the king. 'Maybe, by looking forward together, we can begin to shape a harmonious future for the both of us.' The queen asked the king 'How can we have a harmonious future together?' For a moment the king thought. 'The stones are yours' he said, 'the pastures are ours. Yet we both want what the other has. Maybe we could share. Maybe we could trade. Perhaps we could exchange the produce of our country for the stones of your country. Maybe our people could share their knowledge of farming and your people their knowledge of building. That way we could work together.'

The queen agreed. 'Perhaps' she suggested 'we may even relax the restrictions on the border. Maybe you and your subjects could cross into my country and we into yours. We could trade freely and share what we have to offer each other and exchange our knowledge.'

The countries became the envy of other nations for the way they lived in peace and harmony. True, there were occasions when one desired more stones or the other wanted more produce. That happened from time to time, but now they had a means for resolving differences by understanding, negotiation and trade.

In time, not even an expert geographer would have been able to define where the original boundary had been. There no longer seemed to be any clear dis-

tinction between what had been the stoneless country and the stony country. While maintaining their own unique characters, they had learned to share and exchange what they had with each other.

10 More Solution-Focused Tools

Without forgiveness, there can be no future for a relationship between individuals or within or between nations
Desmond Tutu

Summarizing

In summarizing, the mediator periodically restates to the clients their thoughts, actions, and feelings. It is useful to summarize after the client has given a detailed description of a part of his story. Summarizing reassures the client that the mediator is listening carefully. Words and phrases of the client can be used as a way of respecting the way the clients choose to describe their experiences. Usually summaries have the effect of inviting the clients to say more of what is important to them. They also help the mediator in formulating the next question based on what the clients have just revealed. Successful summarizing requires careful listening, which tends to take heightened emotion out of a discussion or conversation by making differences among participants more rational and understandable. The mediator can either summarize himself or periodically invite the clients to summarize what has been important to them.

Focus on Positive Emotions

Although emotions do not have to be singled out for special conversation in order to build a positive cooperative relationshop with clients, a demonstration of natural, empathic understanding is required and helpful when clients are describing what they find difficult and painful in a given conflict. Empathic affirmation of the client's perspective is useful, "I understand that things have been getting worse between the two of you." Then the mediator can move on to explore what the clients want different in their relationship or what the clients are doing to keep their heads above water.

The focus in solution-focused conflict management is on controling negative emotions and on promoting positive emotions as soon as possible. Macdonald (2007) explains that at the beginning of the meeting, each person may speak once: They may say, "what definitively needs to be said." They may say anything about any topic for as long as they like, but then they have had their say and cannot speak again. They are reminded at the start that criticism of others is likely to draw criticism in return. This method is derived from the Maori people, where the elderly come together to discuss problems and conflicts in their villages.

Fisher and Ury (1981) describe another unusual and powerful technique to control negative emotions: The rules are that only one person at a time is allowed to become angry. The other(s) don't have to react in an angry way: They would say, "Well, now it is his turn, and that is OK." The other advantage is that clients control their emotions better, since they may lose face if they violate these rules.

Others have a large notice on the wall bearing the word "RESPECT." The mediator will point to it when necessary; the nonverbal impact is greater than direct criticism of the speaker. Other participants in the meeting may also point to it rather than responding verbally, which maintains a more amiable level of discourse in the room.

On a recent trip to Mali (West-Africa), I saw that at the heart of every Dogon village is a small structure called a *toguna*. It is the central meeting place for the men of the village, who discuss important matters and swap stories beneath the shaded roof. The short height of the toguna encourages all gathered to sit down and resolve differences and conflicts in the seated position. There is no room to stand up and argue.

In dealing with emotions, it is useful, on one hand, to acknowledge the negative emotions like anger, frustration, or sadness and, on the other hand, to look for possibilities by saying something like, "I see that your feelings are very strong about this topic. What would you like to feel instead in the future when the conflict is solved?"

The transparancy of the mediator's method in a solution-focused approach can also ensure that the potential emotional charge of the focus is reduced. The mediator announces that, together with the clients, he or she will focus on all positive elements that can replace the conflict: What is desirable rather than what is undesirable. This proposal meets with the approval of most clients.

Walter and Peller (2000) state:

Clients sometimes speak only of what they do not want or what they want to eliminate from their lives. In interactional situations, clients often speak of what they want the other person not to do. Their only course of action at that time has been to try to get the other person to stop doing what they consider to be problematic behavior. The other person is also in a strange position, in that the options are either to defend the present behavior or to stop what the other finds so problematic. S/he is still in the dark as to what the client does want to happen. Sometimes, talking about what the client does want opens up the conversation in a more positive direction (p. 124).

Selective attention theory states that what you focus on expands. This theory has obvious applications in relation to emotions. If there is a focus on negative emotions, such as anger, than the anger will increase. Difficulties arise, with the clients becoming increasingly fixated on the obstacles borne of conflict. In areas of neighbor disputes and divorce, where emotions can rapidly escalate, clients will regularly halt the mediation saying, "We have already tried this at home and things didn't improve." An example of this would be the psychoanalytical catharsis method, where there is the assumption that emotions must be aired in order to activate a purifying process, such as is used in transformative mediation.

In solution-focused conflict management, the focus is instead on positive emotions, "How will you feel when your hoped for outcome is reached?" "What will be different for you when you notice that the steps you take are in the right direction?" The broaden-and-build theory (Fredrickson, 2003) as described in Chapter 2, suggests that negative emotions narrow our thought-action repertoires, whereas positive emotions broaden one's awareness and encourage novel, varied, and exploratory thoughts and actions. The power of asking open questions in solution-focused conflict management ("How will you know this meeting has been useful?" "How will you know the conflict has been solved?" "What has been working well?" "What is better?") all serve to widen the array of thoughts and actions. Using imagination, as in the miracle question creates positive emotions and has a powerful impact on our capacity to expand our ideas and activities. While this is highly speculative, it is possible that the miracle question, by engaging our imagery, which is consistent with right hemisphere processing, also engages the global processing capacities of the hemisphere enabling us to expand our thinking. The right hemisphere sees the forest; the left hemisphere sees the trees.

The use of compliments and competence questions ("How did you do that?" "How did you decide to do that?") also elicits positive emotions. The focus of the mediator is on noticing skills and resources of his clients and complimenting or playing those resources back to them.

Isen (2005) states that a growing body of research indicates that positive emotions (happy feelings) facilitates a broad range of important social behaviors and thought processes. For example, work from the past decade shows that positive affect leads to greater creativity, improved negotiation processes and outcomes, and more thorough, open-minded, flexible thinking, and problem solving. And this is in addition to earlier work showing that positive affect promotes generosity and social responsibility in interpersonal interactions.

In a negotiation study, positive affect induced by a small gift (a pad of paper) and a few cartoons significantly increased the tendency of bargainers who were face-to-face to reach agreement and to obtain the optimal outcome possible for both of them in the negotiation. Isen states, "Relative to control groups, people in positive-affect conditions have better negotiation outcomes and enjoy the task more, and they can take the other person's perspective."

The literature indicates that, under most circumstances, people who are feeling happy are more likely to do what they want to do; they want to do what is socially responsible and helpful and what needs to be done; they enjoy what they are doing more; they are more motivated to accomplish their goals and are more open to information; and they think more clearly. In the case of positive emotions, one of the most clear and distinctive cognitive effects observed is increased flexibility and creativity. This may be mediated by release of the neurotransmitter dopamine. Dopamine may play a role in the effects of positive affect on cognition that have been observed. This *dopamine hypothesis* arose from the observation, at behavioral and cognitive levels, that positive affect fosters cognitive flexibility and the ability to switch perspectives (together with the understanding that dopamine in the anterior cingulate region of the brain enables flexible perspective-taking or set-switching).

Apologies, Forgiveness, and Reconciliation

An apology is more than an acknowledgment of an offense together with an expression of remorse. It is an ongoing commitment by the offending party to change his or her behavior. It is a particular way of resolving conflicts other than arguing over who is bigger and better. It is a powerful and constructive form of conflict resolution, embedded, in modified form, in religion and in the judicial system. It is a method of social healing that has grown in importance as our way of living together on our planet undergoes radical change. It is a social act in which the person, group, or nation apologizing has historically been viewed as weak, but more than ever is now regarded as strong. It is a behavior that requires of both parties attitudes of honesty, generosity, humility, commitment, and courage (Lazare, 2004, p. 107).

Apology is but one word, but it is the one word that can make all the difference for those who need to hear it.

Keeva (2004) states that a simple apology might eliminate the costly and frustrating experience of a trial. He believes that the significant impact of an apology is an often-overlooked means of setting a matter without involving a trial. Keeva poses that those who have become attuned to the role of an apology become aware of the human side of a case, something often overlooked in the course of litigation. He reports that at least two states in the USA (Massachusetts and Georgia) have statutes that encourage what they term as "benevolent gestures." Keeva cites research in the USA that indicates 30% of medical malpractice lawsuits would not have gone to court if the doctors had apologized to the plaintiffs.

The purpose of an apology is primarily to help an injured client heal. Noting that in matters of litigation, it is monetary awards that compensate for harm or injury and that courts do not often instruct an apology to be given. New legislation should allow medical practitioners to apologize to patients and their families without fear of malpractice lawsuits. The experience of acknowledging responsibility and expressing a sincere apology for what happened to a person without this fear of consequences is a fair response to wrongdoing. Providing apologies might completely replace the option of seeking justice through litigation, but might offer an altrnative to the adversarial process for those who seek recognition and remorse to feel justice is served.

When offering apologies we recognize the pain of the other, so the relationship can improve. Especially in situations where the relationship continues, it can be an important instrument. Sometimes offering apologies is seen as a sign of weakness. People blame themselves for what has happened, but do not dare to admit it, because it can be used against them. Moreover, they are often afraid of losing face. The mediator could tell clients that the offering of apologies can not be used as a weapon against the other or as evidence.

In *restorative justice*, the making of excuses by the offender is considered important. The key motive of the offender to work with this form of *victim-offender mediation* is taking responsibility, expressing regret, and offering apologies to the victim. Incidentally, the solution-focused professional will rather talk about a *survivor* than a victim, given the passivity associated with the word victim. In order to survive, action is needed (Bannink, 2006a). There are different levels of apologies (from low to high):

- A confession in which the offender acknowledges what they have done. There is no expression of guilt, the offender only says, "I did it."
- A confession that is combined with an expression of guilt. The offender shows sincere regret in word and action. They say, "I did it and I am sorry."
- A confession of guilt and expression of remorse, in which the offender tells how the crime has affected and changed them, so they lead a better life. The offender says, "I did it. I am sorry and it will never happen again." The offender should clearly show that they have changed their life.
- A confession, expressing guilt, remorse and the addition of justice. The offender asks, "What can I do to make up again?" What is perceived as justice may vary.

The offender's expression of shame, remorse or empathic distress was found to be essential for forgiveness.

Sometimes a client demands excuses from the other(s) before he is prepared to continue the mediation. At what level he demands excuses may vary. Remememember that the client who demands excuses is a *complainant*: He wants the other to take the first step.

When the other person is prepared to offer excuses, there is no problem. When the other person is not prepared to offer excuses, the mediation might end in deadlock. Solution-focused questions that may be useful are:

- Suppose the other apologizes, what would change between the two of you?
- What difference would that make?
- What would you be doing differently?
- How would the other react?
- Suppose the other will not apologize, how could you still go on to reach your preferred future?
- How could apologizing help you to collaborate better in the future?
- What are you hoping for when asking for apologies?

Case

Four medical specialists in a partnership are having a conflict. The conflict is about their working schedule, the financial resources, and the treatment of patients. The conflict has lasted for some months already and is rapidly escalating. One of the specialists has even written a letter to their patients about the alleged poor performance of his colleagues. It is, however, clear that they want to continue working together, since they need each other beause of their respective specializations.

The mediation consists of one meeting of 3 hours. To restore a good collaboration (the shared goal of the mediation), they consider it to be important that they offer each other apologies for all that happened. The mediator asks how this will improve their cooperation. They reply that with the offering of apologies, part of the (emotional) damage done could be restored. Two specialists refuse initially, but later are willing to offer their apologies. The mediator's question that helped them overcome this was, "Suppose you were to offer apologies, what difference would that make?" They think their cooperation would be a lot better and so they finally look each other in the eye and shake hands.

Now that the ice is broken, they collectively identify what the new cooperation should look like and what is needed to achieve that objective. For the financial problems and the working schedule, new agreements are made. They also discuss what could and should be better in the treatment of their patients. A full explanatory letter is written and sent to every patient offering apologies.

A short follow-up meeting takes place after four months. One of the specialists has left the partnership and the three remaining doctors are looking for a new colleague. Fortunately, only a few patients have decided to look elsewhere for help and the partnership is functioning well again.

Forgiveness is an important corrective to avoidance and revenge, people's typical negative responses to interpersonal transgressions. For milennia, the world's great religious traditions have commended forgiveness as:

- A response with redemptive consequences for transgressors and their victims;
- A human virtue worth cultivating;
- A form of social capital that helps social units such as marriages, families, and communities operate more harmoniously.

The extent to which an offender apologizes and seeks forgiveness for a transgression also influences victims' likelihood of forgiving. By and large, the effects of apologies appear to be indirect. They appear to cause reductions in victims' negative affect toward their transgressors and increases in empathy for their transgressors. Victims also form more generous impressions of apologetic transgressors. Perhaps apologies and expressions of remorse allow the victim to distinguish the personhood of the transgressor from his or her negative behaviors, thereby restoring a more favorable impression and reducing negative interpersonal motivations (McCullough & vanOyen Witvliet, 2005, p. 450).

Cloke (2006) states that every conflict leads to two different crossroads. In the beginning, there is a choice between fighting and problem solving. Later, there is a subtler, more arduous, and far-reaching choice between merely settling conflicts and seeking to learn from them, correcting behaviors, and moving toward forgiveness and reconciliation. Cloke states that we can forgive our opponents, and finally ourselves. Forgiveness consists of releasing ourselves from the burden of our own false expectations, *giving up all hopes of having a better past.* Forgiveness is a sweeping transformation of the conflict, and few mediators are skilled in methods of reaching forgiveness, especially when it comes to forgiving ourselves. We can reconcile with our opponents and renew our relationships. In reconciliation, we come full circle and our conflicts disappear. At the highest level of reconciliation, conflicts become powerful sources of learning, fresh synthesis, and higher order relationships.

Forgiveness is for the forgiver, not for the perpetrator. In forgiveness, the desire for revenge or punishment is given up, as well as resentment and negative evaluations. The wish or hope that the past can be changed is abandoned. It involves a decision to reduce negative feelings, thoughts, and actions toward the offender(s). Forgiveness is an internal process, not requiring anyone else. It may also create the possibility of renewing positive thoughts, feelings, and actions toward the other(s). Out of this renewal comes the possibility of *reconciliation* (see Chapter 17).

Also on a national level, the possibility of reconciliation can play an important role.

After the end of Apartheid in South Africa, the Truth and Reconciliation Commission (TRC), a court-like body, was assembled. Anybody who felt he had been a victim of violence could come forward and be heard at the TRC. Perpetrators of violence could also give testimony and request amnesty from prosecution. The TRC was seen by many as a crucial component of the transition to full and free democracy in South Africa and, despite some flaws, is generally regarded as successful (Bannink, 2008b).

Not every culture is a forgiving one. In many western cultures, a confession brings immediate absolution. Even leaders apologize for things they did wrong. In China, however, apologies are rarely offered and rarely accepted, because they require a great loss of face. A Chinese lawyer, therefore, founded an apology company who will send a person to apologize on your behalf. These apologizers deliver gifts, make explanations, and write letters.

The legal system can also provide barriers to apology. Lawyers and clients may fear that an admission of culpability can be used against them in court. And for good reason, because only some states and countries prohibit the expressions of sympathy or apology from being used as evidence in a later civil suit.

"I Don't Know"

If clients say "I don't know," there are several reactions possible. The mediator may ask, "Suppose you did know, what would you say?" or, "Suppose you did know, what might be different?" Often clients use this expression as a filler to give them time to think of answers. Given the chance, they will often come up with something useful, when the mediator doesn't do anything for about 6 seconds. About 75% of the clients will start developing an answer within 6 seconds. Or the mediator may ask, "Suppose I was to ask your partner (children, colleagues, best friend), what would they say? Would they be surprised? Which person you know would be least surprised?"

When clients comment that the questions you ask are tough, agree with them and say, "Yes, I am asking you some tough questions. Please take your time."

The mediator may ask themself, "Is it important to my client to know?" They may ask their client, "How would your life be different if you did know?" "How would your life be better if you did know?" They may even say, "Take a guess!" or, "Of course you don't *know* yet, what do you think?" Using these interventions, the facial expression of the mediator should be one of hopeful curiosity.

Arguments

There are cases where clients quarrel during the meeting or continue to quarrel and are not able to stop. Most clients and mediators only look to one side of the coin: How did the quarrel begin? The other side, how they may end the quarrel, is usually overlooked. When clients become more aware, through the mediator's questions of their ability to stop the quarrel and no longer persist in their usual pattern of arguing, then that insight being exceptional to the conflict provides something to build upon .

Solution-focused tips for mediators whose clients who (continue to) quarrel:

- Explain that mediation is not couples therapy. It should be noted that, in couples therapy, an emphasis on arguing is not necessary. The same solution-focused interventions used in conflict management can be successfully used in couples therapy.
- Ask, "Now that you showed me how you start an argument, will you please tell me more about how to stop one?"
- Explain that mediation is costly and that clients would, therefore, be better off quarrelling outside the mediator's office.
- Slide your seat back, indicating that you will no longer be involved in the conversation (see Chapter 15).
- Leave the room, have a cup of coffee, and come back when the clients are ready.
- Say, "Thank you for showing me how you quarrel. I have seen enough, you may as well stop now."
- Say, "Take all the time you need. I see this is very important to you." Usually clients will stop their arguments rather quickly.
- Ask, "In what way will arguing at this table help you reach your goal?"
- Ask, "How do you usually stop an argument? Could that be useful right now?"

Moreover, the mediator can become angry or pretend they are angry. During a lengthy mediation on the distribution of fishing waters in the USA (The Fishing Rights Dispute) between the government and a number of Indian tribes, the mediator decided to lock up the participants and to pretend she was very angry. She told those present that the almost-reached agreement would be lost if they would not stop quarreling. The participants had to decide immediately whether they wanted the agreement or not. She walked out of the room "angrily." It worked out fine: The final agreement was drawn up soon afterwards (Susskind & Cruiksshank, 1987).

Externalization of the Conflict

Externalization of the conflict can help clients see the conflict as something separate from themselves that affects them, but does not always control every aspect of their lives. This intervention was retrieved from the narrative therapy by White and Epston (1990). They granted their clients, with the externalization of the conflict, the freedom to separate themselves from their problematic self-image. In asking how the problem affected their lives and relationships, they offered their clients the opportunity to gain more control. The conflict can be seen as a problem that lies outside the clients and usually has a negative influence on them. The conflict is then seen as an "enemy" by both clients and the mediator and can be fought jointly.

De Shazer (1984) stated that professional and client(s) should be as tennis players on the same side of the net, with the problem or conflict as the opponent. Externalizing the conflict can also be brought about by drawing it or designing a symbol for it. Clients first give a name to the conflict like conflict, srgument, quarrel, or tension. A noun (X) is best for this. The question to the clients is, "How would you name the conflict that bothers you?" Then questions are asked about the times when the conflict (X) is not there or is less (exceptions) and what clients do to bring that about. Clients can also be asked to talk about the times when X is present and how they deal with it. Depending on the needs of the clients more or less time can be spent on finding out how X controls their lives. The competence of the clients can be highlighted and their confidence increased now that more control is possible. Also, the tendency to aportion blame to the other(s) for the conflict can be minimized, as they reap the benefits of collaboration in gaining control over X.

During each meeting, clients can indicate on a scale of 10 to 0 the extent to which the conflict (X) has control over them. The number 10 means the conflict has complete control over them and 0 means they have complete control over X. It is apparent that, in most cases, the conflict will more or less disappear as the control of the clients increases. Solution-focused scaling questions in externalizing the conflict are:

- "On what mark on the scale 10 to 0 are you today?"
- "What was the mark in the previous week/the previous meeting?"
- If the mark is higher than last week/the last meeting, "How did you succeed in doing that?"
- If the mark is the same as the mark for last week/the last meeting, "How did you manage to maintain the same mark?"
- If the mark is lower that last week/ the last meeting, "What did you do earlier to go ahead again?" or "What have you done in the past in a similar situation that has been successful?"
- "What have significant others in your life noticed about you in the last week? How did that influence their behavior towards you?"
- "What are you doing together when X has control over you?"
- "How does X manage to do that?"
- "What do you do (differently) when you have control over X?"
- "What do you do when you are planning to attack X?"
- "How are you able to fool X?"

For externalization of the problem/conflict, see Appendix 4.

■ Exercise 14

Think of a current personal problem or conflict. Ask yourself the above questions. What name would you give the problem or conflict? Discover where you are already on the scale of control: What is already working in the right direction and how you may reach a higher mark.

Spacing Meetings

Traditional mediation models schedule one or more sessions regularly every week or every two weeks. In solution-focused conflict management, each meeting is scheduled according to:
- Time needed for the performance of some home work assignment;
- Promotion of confidence in the solutions;
- Promotion of independence from mediation;
- The client's responsibility for mediation.

Some homework assignments take more time to do or to perceive a meaningful difference for the clients. Spacing out the meetings enables the clients to have a longer perspective on their construction of solutions and to put setbacks in perspective. The spacing of meetings over longer periods of time, from two weeks to three to six, can also promote confidence in solving the conflict, since some clients think that their changing is dependant on mediation and that the mediator is responsible for the change. The spacing of meetings is mostly determined by the clients and not by the mediator by asking questions like, "Do you think it is useful to schedule another meeting?" and, if so, "When would you like to return?" Clients are responsible for their mediation and the solution-focused mediator determines with his clients the amount of time they should be spending on a homework assignment or the length of time between the current and the subsequent meeting, based on the confidence the clients have in their solutions.

Metaphors

The Greek term *metaphor* means to "carry something across" or to "transfer." A metaphor is a figure of speech in which a comparison is made between two things, based on resemblance or similarity, without using "like" or "as." Metaphors enliven ordinary language, encourage interpretation, and are more efficient than ordinary language, because they give maximum meaning with a minimum of words. They imply rather than state relationships and can get clients to think about what they are hearing. Just about any word or phrase can be used as a metaphor.

Sometimes clients will talk about their conflict using a metaphor. They may say, "We are stuck," or "There is an icy atmosphere in this team." The solution-focused mediator may then invite the clients to think of another, more positive metaphor: What would they like to have instead of the negative metaphor?

When clients do not come up themselves with a metaphor, the mediator may introduce this concept and invite clients to think about their conflict in this way. How would they depict the conflict? Team members once described their team as a stony and cold desert. Moving was difficult because of the conflict, and nobody was caring for the others anymore. When the mediator asked the team members which metaphor they would rather have instead in the future, they came up with the metaphor of a boat, floating on a beautiful lake in summer. The mediation continued using this positive metaphor. Were there times in the past when the team had been functioning as a boat on a lake in summer? Which steps could they take to get closer to this image? The team members decided to make a painting together of their ideal boat on the lake and hang the painting in the meeting room for all to see and to remind them every day of their preferred future.

Metaphors are an accurate description of the clients' way of being in the world. The technique of *clean language* (Tompkins & Lawley, 2003) can be applied to discover how clients use metaphors and, if they wish, what needs to happen for them to change so that they have a different perception of the world.

Consensus-Building

Consensus-building is a facilitated or mediated process intended to enable multiple parties to reach agreement without voting. All those who have a stake in the outcome aim to reach agreement on actions and outcomes that resolve or advance issues. Participants work together to design a process that maximizes their ability to resolve their differences. Although they may not agree with all aspects of the agreement, consensus is reached if all participants are willing to live with the total package. It provides an opportunity to work together as equals without imposing the views or authority of one group over another.

Consensus-building means that a number of people with different interests meet together *prior* to the final decision on a specific topic to develop a plan together. This is different from regular mediation, where clients reach an agreement *afterwards*.

It is mostly used in disputes where the government is involved. The usual top-down decision-making, where the order is decide, announce, and defend has often led to resistance among the population.

Consensus-building was created in the eighties in the context of environmental issues. The advantage of bringing together interested people to make a proposal is that is usually leads to a greater commitment and responsibility felt for the final result. A broader coalition gives a better basis for the realization of these proposals.

Susskind and Cruikshank (1987): "One of the most exciting aspects of consensual approaches to dispute resolution is that once people use them, and find that they work, those people become advocates" (p. 247). They describe the problem solving variant of consensus-building, where the use of caucus at the beginning of the negotiation process is seen as crucial.

In consensus-building, often many (groups of) clients are participating. In disputes with the government, sometimes more that 100 groups and individuals can be involved.

> Our experience suggests that it is always better to include too many people or groups than too few – especially at the outset. There is a logistical advantage, of course, in limiting the number of voices directly involved in consensus-building discussions. That advantage is far outweighed, however, by the problems that arise if someone decides they have been unfairly excluded (Susskind & Cruikshank, 1987, p. 101).

The Harmon County Sewage Clean-up in the U.S. was for twelve years a heated dispute over sewage in the US. The city Harmon refused a particularly high financial contribution for this project. The negotiations failed because almost everyone involved in the court was asked whether they were *completely satisfied* with the ultimate agreement. This question received many negative reactions. In this case, the judge might better have asked whether anyone could *reasonably live with the agreement.*

Consensus building is similar to mediation in a number of aspects. The rules of the third neutral person, voluntary participation, equal contribution, and fair procedure are also applicable here. Because of the public nature of issues concerning the government, privacy – or confidentiality – are usually not possible.

Solution-Focused Consensus-Building

In solution-focused consensus-building, the mediator will ask all participants to anticipate the preferred future. First, a mutual goal will be developed and then they will work backward to the here and now. Solution-focused questions for consensus-building are:
- Can you describe how you want the situation to be in about 1-year's time (or any other relevant period), when everything goes well (or is better)?
- What has been done to achieve this?
- Who has helped to achieve this?
- What have they done exactly?
- What have you done to get to this point?
- Where did you get those good ideas?
- What else have you done to contribute to achieve this?

- What did you worry about a year ago, looking back on today?
- What has helped to reduce or to minimize these worries?

The mediator summarizes the answers to the questions above and on the basis of all suggestions given, designs the preferred future of the participants. Then, there is further discussion on the proposed plan. Susskind and Cruikshank mention five questions to which an affirmative answer must be given before consensus-building may be considered:

- Can the key players be identified, and if so, can the mediator convince them that it is in their interest to talk with each other?
- Is the power sufficiently balanced?
- Can the mediator find a legitimate spokesman for each group?
- Are there deadlines? Are they realistic?
- Can the mediator reformulate the dispute so that there are no fundamental values at stake?

If there are very many people involved and/or if it is a very complex problem, the mediator can use a variation of consensus-building for a *minimal plan*. Solution-focused questions for a minimal plan are:

- What will happen if you do nothing?
- Suppose you would like to do something to help, what could that be?
- What would be your minimum input?
- What would happen when you do that?
- What could be the next (small) step?
- Who will take the next step with whom and when will that be?

11 Team Mediation

A conflict is a situation, which needs a design effort
Edward de Bono

Case

The team consists of six nurses in an institution for people with psychiatric problems. There has been a bad atmosphere within the team for two years. This developed following a severe accident involving a resident, due to accusations of negligence within the group leading to a lack of mutual trust. Attempts to restore good cooperation within the team have failed. The director has spoken with all team members and has appointed a coach from within the institution. Since there has been no improvement, the director has sent the team to an external mediator. If there is still no improvement, dismissals are likely to occur. The nurses have agreed to mediation, albeit reluctantly.

The first meeting starts with preliminary introductions and the creation of a positive, informal atmosphere through agreeing to continue on a first name basis, with the mediator showing an interest in the clients' working and private lives and giving compliments for the courage to start the mediation. Then follows an explanation of the solution-focused mediation process: the conversation will not so much focus on the conflict itself as it will on what they would like to see different: their preferred future as a team and on how that may be achieved. There is room for acknowledging their emotions and normalizing the frustration by reacting with empathy to the brief history of the conflict. The clients are given space to say "what definitely needs to be said." Some make use of this by expressing the hope that these meetings will lead to a positive result. Others explain shortly to the mediator what has happened in the past. Following this, the mediator asks the goal formulation questions, "What is your best hope?" and "What difference would that make?"

All team members indicate that they would like to cooperate in a pleasant manner again, with a restoration of mutual trust. This would result in greater pleasure at being part of the team. The mediator inquires into concrete behavior and how that would manifest itself, "How could you tell that the level of trust between you was increasing? What would you be doing differently?" Because most team members initially think others, rather than themselves need to change (assessing motivation: complainant-relationship), the mediator asks, "Suppose the behavior of the others is more in line with the desired direction, what would you personally do differently?" The mediator asks, "What is already working towards your preferred future? What else?" Then the progress is scaled, "On a scale of 10 to 0 (10 = pure cooperation and 0 = pure conflict), where would you say you are right now?" The nurses mention marks between 2 and 5. The scale of 10 to 0 is drawn as a vertical line on a flip chart and the marks are applied to this. The mediator asks every member how they have already succeeded in reaching that mark and gives compliments. In addition, the mediator asks the team members which mark they would like to attain: Which mark is good enough? All would like to achieve at least a 7 or 8. The next questions are, "What will one mark higher from now look like and what would you then be doing differently?" "How might you reach this mark?" "What would be the next step?" and, "How would your colleagues notice that you have achieved one mark higher?" The team members are also asked how their patients and their director would notice that they as a team are progressing towards a 7 or 8 (*relationship questions*).The mediator gives feedback: compliments for the willingness to improve the team atmosphere and the concrete steps mentioned to reach one mark higher. At the end of the meeting all team members are invited to pay attention until the next meeting to the moments when the team has already (for a while) reached one mark higher, so that next time this can be discussed. The final question is, "Do you think it is useful to return?" The team members specify the scheduling of the next appointment.

The opening question in the second meeting ten days later is, "What is better?" The team members say that things are going slightly better. They talk more to each other and the air seems to have cleared a little; they also greet each other again in the corridor. They are invited to give details about how they were able to do this and the mediator compliments them with the achieved result. Again, scaling questions are used. The marks are a little higher, ranging from a 4 to a 6.5. Again, the marks are recorded on the flip chart. The team members explain how they have reached these marks. The team meetings are becoming more constructive because they do not interrupt each other and listen more to one another. The next questions are, "What might one mark higher from now look like?" "What would be the next step?" "What would you be doing differently?" and "What can you do yourself and what do you need from the other team members?" At the end of this meeting, the feedback consists of compliments from the mediator and the suggestion, "When you work together in the weeks to come, act as if you are already one mark higher and take notice of what difference that makes. The mediator asks, "Do you think it is useful to return and if so, when should the next appointment take place?"

The opening question in the third and final meeting, four weeks later, is, "What is better?" All indicate that it is going fairly well. Marks range from 5.5 to 8. Again, they are recorded on the flip chart. The mutual trust has, to some extent, been restored. They have become more interested in each other and increasingly enjoy each other's company. Included in the settlement agreement is the intention to work as much as possible as a *dream team*. Should, despite their best efforts, a new dispute arise, they will again attempt to find solutions through mediation. To conclude, the mediator compliments the team with the achieved result. Following this meeting, the team members sign the settlement agreement. They decide to have dinner together as way of celebration. Four months after signing the agreement, a follow-up by telephone finds that the team – and the director – are satisfied with the result.

■ Exercise 15

Let your team demonstrate a typical meeting, with some team members acting as observers who count the problem-focused comments. Then, after a few minutes, ask the team to change to a solution-focused conversation, with the comments being counted in the same way. The count will demonstrate the differences between the two types of conversations and how easy it is to slip back into problem-focused talk, while the team members will usually report a preference for the solution-focused conversation.

Game Theory Revisited: Trust

By *trust*, I do not refer to the fact that clients are confident that they will achieve their goal. This kind of confidence and how to increase it is discussed in Chapter 6. Also, the trust that clients have in the mediator and the mediation process is not discussed here, except that the question of trust in the mediator, in my view, can only be answered by the clients themselves, with whom the mediator has collaborated.

The concept of trust is described by Lewicki and Wiethoff (2000). They describe the concept of trust, trust development, and trust repair. They state that mutual trust is the glue that links people together. Their definition of trust is, "An individual's belief in, and willingness to act on the basis of, the words, actions, and decisions of another" (p. 87). Sharing a common goal is, in their view, one of the ways to build mutual trust.

Susskind and Cruikshank (1987) argue that it is unrealistic to ask clients to trust each other: Trust must be earned. The overriding consideration of each client to trust the other is reciprocity: Why should I keep my promise if the other doesn't? The mediator must therefore assume that the meetings begin without mutual trust and that mutual trust can only be built if clients behave accordingly.

The *prisoner's dilemma,* as described in Chapter 2, has some key features that have shaped the unfolding of nonzero-sum games during human history. The two key features are communication and trust. It is crucial that when your partner and you assure each other you will stay mum, you believe each other. If you suspect that your partner may renege on the deal, then you are better off repaying his cheating with cheating by copping a plea yourself: a three-year prison sentence as opposed to a ten-year sentence. And your suspicions are hardly irrational, since your partner does have a temptation to cheat: If he confesses while you honor your deal and stay mum, he gets to walk!

In a tournament, many computer programs were submitted that embodied particular strategies for playing the prisoner's dilemma. These programs could interact with each other and "decide" whether to cheat or to cooperate. In making this decision, the programs would often draw on their memory of how the other program had behaved in the past encounters. The winning program was called *Tit for Tat.* Its strategy was very simple. On its first encounter with any given program, it would cooperate. On subsequent encounters, it would do whatever that program had done on the previous occasion. In short, Tit for Tat would reward past cooperation with present cooperation and would punish past cheating with present cheating. In this way, interactions blossomed into stable, cooperative relationships. It was shown that cooperation could evolve even without formal communication: Reciprocal altruism could evolve in animals that don't do much talking, including chimpanzees and vampire bats.

Pruitt and Kim (2004) state that two problems arise when using Tit for Tat. One results from the fact that immediate retaliation is required from one party, even if the other party has made a momentary mistake. If the other is employing Tit for Tat too, as is often the case, doing so may start an unnecessary conflict spiral in an otherwise good relationship. In addition, if the other's failure to cooperate comes at the beginning of their interaction, the other may never learn that good behavior pays off. Instead, the other may develop an incorrect view of the other party as a nasty creature who never cooperates and should be avoided and disciplined. As the solution to this problem, they state that this problem can be avoided if the party gives the other party a grace period, continuing to behave positively for a while in response to the other's unpleasant behavior. Including a warning during this grace period is often effective. Another solution to this problem is for the party to explain Tit for Tat in words: I can be nice if you work with me instead of against me.

The second problem with Tit for Tat is that its effectiveness is often limited to the period in which it is employed. The cooperative behavior of the other party is likely to taper off if the first party stops using the tactic. It is found that the effect of Tit for Tat lasts longer after the tactic is discontinued if the other party had been rewarded for cooperation intermittently rather than every time.

In sum, as Scheinecker (2006) states, "The solution-focused approach has shown to be highly fruitful in all situations where a change of perceptions, evaluations, feelings, and needs or goals can contribute to de-escalation" (p. 323).

Kelman (2006) mentions the dilemma of building mutual trust that enemies such as the Israelis and Palestinians face: How can you work on the peace process if there is no mutual trust and how can you build mutual trust if the peace process does not even start? The answer is located in designing small steps to reach the mutual goal (successive approximation of commitment and reassurance, p. 644).

Useful solution-focused questions are:

- What did the other say or do that gave you the idea that they want a solution to the conflict?
- What has given you the idea that the other understands you, even just a little bit?
- Suppose there were more mutual trust between you, what would change or what would be different in your relationship with the other?
- How could more mutual trust help you to achieve your preferred future?
- If 10 means the mutual trust is optimal, and 0 means there is no mutual trust at all, what mark would you give right now?
- How did you achieve this mark? Why is it not less?
- What would one mark higher on the scale look like? What would be different between the two of you?
- What small steps are possible to reach a higher mark?
- How can you contribute to this higher mark?
- What would you be doing differently?
- What would you need from the other to reach a higher mark?

"Liquid Trust"

Oxytocin is a nine-amino-acid peptide that is synthesized in hypothalamic neurons and transported down axons of the posterior pituitary for secretion into blood. Oxytocin receptors are expressed by neurons in many parts of the brain and spinal cord, including the amygdala, ventromedial hypothalamus, septum, and brain stem. Oxytocin is released in response to stress, touch, and during breastfeeding. It has a role in social behaviors in many species and it seems likely that it has similar roles in humans. Oxytocin promotes the secretion of breast milk and stimulates the contraction of the uterus during labor. It increases trust and reduces fear and is often called the "tend and befriend" hormone (Cloke, 2009).Animals prefer to spend time with animals in whose presence they have experienced high brain oxytocin in the past, suggesting that friendships may be mediated at least in part by the same system that mediates maternal urges.

In one study, volunteers were asked to play to types of games: a trust game and a risk game. In the trust game, subjects were asked to contribute money, with the understanding that a human trustee would invest the money and decide whether to return the profits, or betray the subjects' trust and keep all the money. In the risk game, the subjects were told that a computer would randomly decide whether their money would be repaid or not. The subjects also received doses of either oxytocin or a placebo via nasal spray. They chose oxytocin because studies had shown that oxytocin specifically increases people's willingness to trust others. During the games the subjects' brains were scanned using functional magnetic resonance imaging.

The researchers found that – in the trust game, not in the risk game – oxytocin reduced activity in two brain regions: the amygdala, which processes fear, danger, and possibly risk of social betrayal, and an area of the striatum, part of the circuitry that guides and adjusts future behavior based on reward feedback. Baumgartner and his colleagues (2008) concluded that their findings showed that oxytocin affected the subjects' responses specifically related to trust. If subjects face the nonsocial risks in the risk game, oxytocin does not affect their behavioral responses to the feedback. Both subjects in the oxytocin group and the placebo group do not change their willingness to take risks after the feedback. In contrast, if subjects face social risks, such as in the trust game, those who received placebo respond to the feedback with a decrease in trusting behavior while subjects with oxytocin demonstrate no change in their trusting behavior although they were informed that their interaction partners did not honor their trust in roughly 50% of the cases.

Nasally administered oxytocin has also been reported to reduce fear, possibly by inhibiting the amygdala (which is thought to be responsible for fear response). Its effect lasts only for a few minutes though. Oxytocin also affects generosity by increasing empathy during perspective-taking. In experiments, intranasal oxytocin increased generosity, but had no effect onaltruism. Oxytocin, also named *liquid trust,* can be bought as a nasal spray. Maybe mediators could use the spray to help clients to trust each other more than they usually do when starting mediation? Or maybe that is why a handshake (touching releases oxytocin) can be so important in mediation.

The Price to Pay

Cloke (2001) states that when we recognize that conflicts can teach us unique and important lessons and contain secrets that can transform our lives, suddenly the price of conflict is transformed into an immense sourse of value, allowing us to free ourselves from conflict's icy grip, release our spirits, and open our hearts. He sees conflict as simply a place where people are stuck and unable to be relaxed and authentic, and by learning to become unstuck, they can discover how to transcend not only that conflict, but other conflicts as well.

He asks his clients many useful questions to "expand heart spaces in mediation." Some are about the price the clients pay for the conflict:

- What issues are you holding onto that the other person still does not know about?
- What have you been holding onto that it is now time to release?
- What is the price you have to pay for the conflict you are in?
- How much longer are you going to continue paying that price?
- What would it take for you to give this conflict up, let go of what happened, and move on with your life?
- Do you really want this in your life? What would it take to let it go?

Story 9: Finding Peace

One evening, a couple strolled along a beach, found a peaceful spot to spread their rug and nestled down to watch the sunset. They brought a chicken picnic and a bottle of fruity, dry wine with them. He poured the wine and toasted their happiness. She spread out the picnic. The scene was peaceful and romantic, but they were not alone.

The woman looked at the flock of begging seagulls and threw her last piece of meat into its midst. One gull could not believe its luck. It opened its beak and launched itself at the piece of meat. Wings beat about it in a desperate flutter. Discordant shrieking pierced the air. Dozens of birds swooped at the small morsel – and the first gull won. It wheeled urgently into the air, turning toward open sea and sky, but the other gulls did not give up. In hot pursuit, twenty or so birds began their greedy attacks. There was no mercy in their relentless struggle to get it. Some tried to snatch the piece of meat from the bird's mouth. Others, seeming to have forgotten the object of their desire, attacked the gull itself. They screeched at it, flew at it, and pecked at it, but the gull flew on. It had acquired the piece of chicken in fair play, fortune had bestowed it with this gist, and it wasn't about to give up what it had won.

But the battle was not over. The other gulls were also reluctant to give up. Temptation was in their sight, and they wanted the prize. It grew harder and harder for the winning gull to hang on to the piece of chicken. Finally, feeling the exhaustion and fatigue of trying to fight against the odds, the gull began to question whether it was worth hanging on. What price did it have to pay to keep this piece of meat? Was it really worth the effort?

At some stage the gull realized there would come a time when it had to let go of what it had been hanging on to. There would come a point where the consequences of the struggle outweighed the benefits of the reward. It opened its beak, let the piece of chicken fall, and watched as another bird darted below to snatch up the morsel. Its attackers swiftly found their new target, the battle moved to a different field, and the gull felt relieved.

It remembered a saying that sea birds liked to repeat: There are plenty more fish in the ocean. It knew that it would not go hungry or be deprived. It knew its own skills at hunting and was aware of the opportunities that awaited it. With the battle behind, it was free to tame its own time to look leisurely for another meal. Now it had a choice of where and when it sought out the things that would nurture, satisfy, and make it happy. The battle was not necessary for its survival. Once more it wheeled in the air. This time it was not to avoid attack, just purely for fun. It soared up on the refreshing sea breeze, a contrasting dot of liberated whiteness in the rich blue of the sky. The gull enjoyed its freedom and peace.

The couple, sitting on the beach for their sunset picnic, watched as a lone seagull separated itself from the crowd of squabbling birds. They followed its silhouette as it drifted leisurely across the golden rays of the setting sun. They embraced, feeling the serenity and intimacy that accompanies a day as it draws to a close. The seagull, too, felt at one with the tranquillity of its world. It thought to itself 'I may have lost a piece of meat, but I have gained the peace of the sky'.

12 Client-Directed, Outcome-Informed Conflict Management

> *Until lions have their historians, tales of hunting will always*
> *glorify the hunter*
> African proverb

Suppose you are both hungry and decide to eat in a restaurant. After having waited for some time, you are invited to take a seat and the manager introduces himself. He asks you many questions regarding your hunger: 'How hungry are you? For how long have you been preoccupied with this feeling? Were you hungry in the past? What role did hunger play earlier in your life? What disadvantages and possibly advantages does hunger have for you?' After this, having become even hungrier, you ask if you can now eat. Then a meal is served to you that you did not order, but that the manager claims is good for you and has helped other hungry people. What are the chances of you both leaving the restaurant feeling satisfied?

Client-Directed Conflict Management

Miller et al. (1996) collected data from forty years of outcome research in psychotherapy, which provide strong empirical evidence for privileging the client's role in the change process. Duncan et al. (2004) state that clients, not therapists, make therapy work. As a result, therapy should be organized around their resources, their perceptions, their experiences and their ideas. There need be no *a priori* assumptions about client problems or solutions, no special questions that are best to ask, and no invariant methodology to follow to achieve success. Rather, therapists need only take directions from clients: following their lead; adopting their language, worldview, goals, and ideas about the conflict; and acknowledging their experiences with, and inclinations about, the change process. The most potent factor of successful outcome, the client and his own propensities for change, are left out from the medical model. It is the client who is the director of the change endeavor, not the mediator.

Traditionally, the effectiveness of treatment has been left up to the judgement of the provider of this treatment. But proof of effectiveness can emerge from the client's perception and experience as a full partner in the mediation process.

The client's theory of change offers ways of integrating many perspectives on mediation. Trusting the client's theory of change requires a focused effort to conduct mediation within the context of the client's unique ideas and circumstances. Research has shown that all model and technique factors only represent 15% of outcome variance at most. They may or may not be useful in the client's circumstances. Therefore, theories should be deemphasized and instead the focus should be on the clients' theories. Exploring their ideas has several advantages:

- It puts the clients center stage in the conversation;
- It enlists the clients' participation;
- It helps ensure the clients' positive experience of the professional;
- It structures the conversation and directs the change process.

According to research, it is the client that matters: his resources, participation, evaluation of the alliance, and his perceptions of the conflict and the resolution. The mediator's techniques are only helpful if the client sees them as relevant and credible.

If, for example, it is the clients' theory of change that it is useful to talk at length about who is guilty and is to blame, the mediator may ask:

- How do you think this will be helpful?
- What are your ideas about the positive effects this will have on your preferred future?
- How may your relationship with the other(s) benefit from this?
- How will you know this will be helpful for you? What needs to be better the next time we meet, so we know this has been useful and we should do more of it?

Outcome-Informed Conflict Management

Conventional wisdom suggests that competence engenders, if not equals, effectiveness. As a result, there is a continuing education requirement, designed to ensure that mediators stay abreast of developments that enhance positive outcome of mediation. The vast majority of these trainings do not include any methods for evaluating the effectiveness of the approach. Emphasis is placed on learning skills or techniques of a particular brand or style of mediation.

But this emphasis on competence versus outcome decreases effectiveness and efficiency. Research showed that there is no or little relationship between the experience level and effectiveness of professionals (Clement, 1994). The data indicate that increasing the amount and type of training and experience that most professionals receive may even lessen their effectiveness. Researchers distinguished successfully between least and most effective therapists as determined by outcome (Hiatt & Hargrave, 1995). They found that therapists in the low-effectiveness group tended to have been in practice for more years that those in the high-effectiveness group. They also found that the ineffective therapists were unaware that they were ineffective. Even worse, they considered themselves as effective as the truly helpful therapists in the study.

Miller et al. (1997) state that using client feedback to inform the professional would invite clients to be full and equal partners in all aspects of mediation. Giving clients the perspective of the driver's seat instead of the back of the bus may also enable them to gain confidence that a positive outcome is just down the road.

Systematic assessment of the client's perceptions of progress and fit are important, so the clinician can empirically tailor the therapy to the client's needs and characteristics. Such a process of becoming outcome-informed fits well with how most therapists prefer to think of themselves: sensitive to client feedback and interested in results. Becoming outcome-informed not only amplifies the client's voice, but also offers the most viable, research-tested method to improve effectiveness (Duncan et al., 2004, p. 16).

They offer the following equation: Client resources and resilience + client theories of change + client feedback about the fit and benefit of service = client perceptions of preferred outcomes.

Session Rating Scale

Apart from asking scaling questions about progress during the mediation sessions, clients can be given the Session Rating Scale (SRS) at the end of every session (see Appendix 5).

The Session Rating Scale is divided into four areas that decades of research have shown to be the qualities of change-producing relationships. Clients are asked to place a mark on each line, where low estimates are represented to the left and high to the right. Each line has a potential of 10, with a grand total possibility of 40. A centimeter ruler can be used to measure the mark of the client on each line and then they can be added up. There is no specific cutoff score between relationships that have good or bad change potential. Higher scores (above 30) reflect relationships that have better change potential, lower scores suggest the relationship may need some extra attention. In this case, it is the mediator who should ask, "What should I (in our work as a mediator, note that the SRS is developed for therapists) do differently next time so you (the client(s)) will give higher marks on the scale.

The SRS is an engagement instrument. There is no magic in the scale itself, it is aimed at starting a conversation with the client, which can be used by the mediator to improve the mediation for this particular client. Dropout rates will be higher if the SRS is forgotten. It is helpful to make a graphic of the results of the SRS over time (for instructions see www.scottdmiller.com). This paints a good picture and gives good feedback to the mediator. A small decrease (1 point) is a signal that the mediator should discuss the relationship with his client.

> Monitoring progress is essential and dramatically improves the chances of success. You don't really need the perfect approach as much as you need to know whether your plan is working – and if it is not, how to quickly adjust your strategy to maximize the possibility of improvement (Duncan, 2005, p. 183).

An absence of early improvement may substantially decrease the chances of achieving what clients want to achieve with the current methods. Research in psychotherapy showed that when no improvement occurred by the third visit, progress was not likely to occur over the entire course of treatment. Moreover, people who did not indicate that therapy was helping by the sixth meeting were very likely to receive no benefit, despite the length of the therapy. The diagnosis the person had and the type of therapy delivered were not as important in predicting success as knowing whether the treatment that was provided was actually working! Studies have found that individuals whose therapists got feedback about their client's lack of progress were, at the conclusion of therapy, better off than 65% of those whose therapists did not receive any information. Just knowing that their clients were not benefiting from their therapy allowed these therapists to modify their approaches and promote change. Clients whose therapists had access to progress information, like the Session Rating Scale, were less likely to get worse with treatment and were *twice as likely* to achieve a clinically significant change. Nothing else in the history of psychotherapy has been shown to increase effectiveness this much.

Becoming outcome-informed is simple and straightforward, also in conflict management. Unlike product-oriented efforts the field has employed so far, outcome management results in significant improvements in effectiveness. Liberated from the traditional focus on models or techniques, professionals would be better able to achieve what they always claimed to have been in the business of doing: assisting change. For the Session Rating Scale and the website address with instructions for use of the SRS see Appendix 5.

13 Family Mediation

A harvest of peace is produced from a seed of contentment
American Proverb

Case

The mediation concerns a father (aged 55, engineer) and his only child (aged 25, sales manager). The father remarried several years ago. The son lives independently and has no partner. There has been no contact between father and son for four years due to an argument. The father makes an appointment by telephone: He wants to explore whether mediation will help and his son has reluctantly agreed. The father hopes that the presence of a mediator will prevent the argument from flaring up again when they speak to each other and also hopes to re-establish long-term contact. Even prior to the argument there was very little contact following the divorce. The son was 11 years old at the time. The mediation took three sessions (a total of four hours) with both clients present.

The first meeting starts with the preliminary introductions and the creation of a positive, informal atmosphere through agreeing to continue on a first name basis, with the mediator showing an interest in the clients' working and private lives and giving compliments for the courage in initiating the mediation and the willingness to find a solution together. Then follows an explanation of the solution-focused mediation process, in which the mediator indicates the structure: the conversation will focus on their mutual goal and on how that may be achieved, ending with feedback from the mediator, including (if they wish) a suggestion for homework to be carried out before the next conversation. There is also room for acknowledging and normalizing the frustration by reacting with empathy to the brief history of the conflict. The mediation agreement is formulated with a general description of the conflict, "conflict regarding the relationship." Father and son decide to divide the costs of the mediation 75/25% because of a difference in income.

Following this, the mediator asks the goal formulation question, "What would you like to have achieved at the end of this mediation to deem the mediation successful?" Both clients reply, "A good relationship, with mutual trust and interest, doing things together and enjoying each other's company." They would like to improve their communication as well. Questions concerning concrete behavior are, "How could you tell that there would be an increase in trust and interest?" and "What could the other person change for you to trust him more?: Scaling questions used were, "Suppose you were to give a mark for the quality or your communication right now, 10 means an optimal communication and 0 means the worst communication imaginable, which mark would you give?" It comes as no surpise that both give very low marks: the father gives a 2, the son a 1. "How come the marks are not lower than this?" asks the mediator. "What would a mark highter on the scale look like?" "What would be different in their communication?"

The mediator asks what they themselves would do differently, supposing that the other's behavior was more in line with the desired direction. And, "What enjoyable things will you be doing together once the relationship and communication has improved?" Assessing motivation: with the father there is a customer relationship, with the son a complainant-relationship; at this point son appears not (yet) to view himself as part of the solution and believes that father is to blame and should change.

The mediator explores the exceptions, "At what times was the conflict there to a lesser extent and who did what in order to encourage these exceptions?" and, "When were there moments that already to some extent resembled the goal you both wish to achieve?" The son recalls moments in the past when he did not feel forgotten by his father, occurring on occasions when they actively did something together. The way in which they talk about the future during the initial conversation is experienced as a beginning of the goal they wish to achieve.

Utilizing scaling questions, "On a scale of 10 to 0 (10 means an excellent relationship and 0 means a very bad relationship), where would you say you are right now?" The father gives a 4, the son a 2.5. "What did you do to reach this mark?" The father answers, "I have always continued to love him and hope that the relationship can improve, although I am also angry because he has not been in touch for four years." The fact that the son has agreed to mediation has made the father hopeful. The son gives a 2.5 because he says he loves his father, too, but feels neglected, due to his father leaving after the divorce and rarely keeping in touch. The next questions are, "What would one mark higher look like and what would you then be doing differently?" and, "How might you reach this mark?" At 5, the father would do something enjoyable together with the son, such as going to a football match; the son would reach a 3 or 3.5 if his father would show more interest in him, for example, by asking how work is going.

Feedback: the mediator gives compliments for the wilingness of both to improve the relationship and the concrete steps they mentioned to reach one mark higher. The mediator gives a suggestion for homework: Both are invited to pay attention to the moments when the relationship has already (for a while) reached one mark higher, so that next time this can be discussed. The final question is, "Do you think it is useful to return?" When the answer is yes, the clients specify the scheduling of the next appointment.

The opening question of the second meeting, seven days later, is, "What is better?" Both say that things are going better; after the last conversation, they went for a drink together on the initiative of the father and he showed an interest in the life and work of his son. The son has brought a file along containing copies of letters (of an angry nature) written to his father in the past. The son suggests discussing the letters in this meeting. The mediator asks, "How would discussing these letters help bring you closer to your goal?" Then, the son realizes that he actually wants his father's recognition for the lack of interest he has experienced and decides to directly confront his father. The father reacts in a positive way, gives his views on the past, and apologizes. The mediator asks whether it is still necessary to discuss the letters. The answer of son is in the negative. And neither of them still thinks it necessary to elaborate further upon the conflict as described in the mediation agreement to achieve the goal (a good relationship). Through these interventions with the son, a customer relationship has evolved: he now sees himself as part of the solution and is motivated to contribute toward the goal.

Utilizing scaling questions, the question as to how they score is answered by the father with a 6 and by the son with a 6.5. They explain how they have reached these marks (for the son, the father's recognition and apologies have clearly been helpful in improving the situation). The next questions are, "What might one mark higher from now look like? What would you then be doing differently and what could you do to achieve this?" The father would give one mark higher if his son would be willing to have more contact with his second wife, but the son refuses this. However, there appear to be other ways to reach one mark higher, for example, if son will visit his father at home one day while his wife is out.

Feedback consists of compliments from the mediator and the following suggestion for homework, "When you see each other in the weeks to come, act as if you are already one mark higher and take notice of any differences to the present situation." The final question is, "Do you think it is useful to return and if so, when should the next appointment take place?"

The opening question in the final meeting, three weeks later, again is, "What is better?" Both indicate that it is now going fairly well. The mark from the father is 7 and, from the son, a 7.5. The son has realized that his father has a life of his own with his second wife and that he does not want to be involved in this. The father has realized that the idea of the three of them doing things together seems, as yet, unfeasible and decides to no longer insist on this. There remain plenty of things to do together. The mutual trust has to some extent been restored; as for the future, "time will tell," say both. They have become more interested in each other and increasingly enjoy each other's company. Included in the settlement agreement is the intention to maintain a good relationship and to stay in touch in the event of an argument. It is also agreed that criticism of each other will be expressed verbally rather than through angry letters. Should, despite their best efforts, a new dispute arise, they will again attempt to find a solution through mediation. In addition, an agreement is made whereby the father, as a token of good will, writes off a sum of money that son still owes him. The son had borrowed the money for driving lessons and buying a second-hand car. Both deem further agreements unnecessary. To conclude, the mediator compliments both for the achieved result and the father and son decide to celebrate the improvement in their relationship with a weekend skiing holiday. Following this meeting, the settlement agreement is sent and signed by both. Three months after signing the settlement agreement, a follow-up by telephone finds that both father and son are doing fine and enjoyed a nice weekend together.

Communication

It is often the desire of clients to enhance their communication. Not only to resolve the existing conflict, but also to be able to overcome future conflicts without the help of a third person like a mediator. Solution-focused questions to enhance communication are:

- Suppose you would (both) give a mark on your communication at this moment, 10 meaning the communication is perfect and 0 meaning the communication is as bad as can be, what mark would you give right now?
- How did you succeed to be at this mark? Why is it not less?
- Suppose the mark would be somewhat higher on the scale, what would be different between the two of you?
- What would you be doing differently?
- How can better communication help you to reach your preferred future?
- What would the other(s) notice that is different when the mark is higher on the scale?
- How can the other(s) help you to reach a higher mark on the scale?
- What can you do to help the other(s) reach a higher mark on the scale?
- At what mark would you be satisfied?

Tolerance

For years, difficulties in relationships have been attributed to poor communication. In response, professionals have focused their efforts on improving communication between partners, especially about problems and the expression of emotion. While effective communication has been linked to marital satisfaction in the research literature, a recent study (Gordon, Baucom, Epstein, Burnett, & Rankin, 1999) suggests a more effective alternative: *teaching tolerance.*

In particular, partners can be helped to become more tolerant (and probably more forgiving) when they adjust their expectations to the type of communication pattern they have. For example, avoidance of discussing problems and sharing emotions had less relation to marital satisfaction and happiness in couples that preferred more emotional and psychological space and less conjoint decision making.

14 Brief Comparison with Other Models

Nothing is more dangerous than an idea if it is the only one you have
Emile Chartier

■ Exercise 16

What do you think are the *three most important questions in mediation*? Or, which three questions do you use most? Write these three questions down to find out what assumptions you have. Look then at the assumptions that underlie your questions, because these assumptions probably contain your personal beliefs about people and about your work as a mediator.

Suppose one of your questions is, "How do you feel?" Then the underlying premise is that the client feels something, the situation is a cause, there is a linear causal link between the situation and the feeling, the client is capable of describing this feeling, and the description of the feeling is somehow useful.

When you have clarified your assumptions, then ask yourself whether the three questions actually relate to what you believe. If that is not the case, what are your ideas about people and about change? And how can you change your questions so that they reflect your ideas in the best possible way?

Building Solutions Is Different from Problem Solving

Building solutions is different from problem solving. According to the cause-and-effect medical model, one should explore and analyze the conflict in order to make a diagnosis, before the remedy can be administered. This model is useful where it concerns relatively simple problems, which can be reduced to uncomplicated and distinct causes for example medical or mechanical problems (in the case of a vacuum cleaner that breaks down). A disadvantage is that this model is problem-focused. If the conflict and its possible causes are studied, a vicious circle may be created with ever increasing problems. The atmosphere becomes loaded with problems, bringing with it the danger of losing sight of the solutions.

> An analysis turns a focal point into a whole field by looking in detail at what has been focused upon and breaking down into even smaller areas each of which can become a point of focus...It must be emphasized that analysis is by no means the whole of thinking, and analysis by itself will not solve problems. In the past rather too much attention has been paid to logical analysis as the only required tool of thinking (De Bono, 1985, p. 171).

Both the problem solving and the transformative model are variations of this cause-and-effect model. The narrative model stands between the solution-focused and the other two models. These four models differ from one another with regard to the mediator's goal and his competencies. Behind these differences lie hidden fundamental ideas about human nature, social interaction, and conflict; in short, differences in ideology.

Baruch, Bush and Folger (2005) state, and I concur, that different models can exist side by side and that they can help clients, as long as there is sufficient transparency about the model employed by the mediator, so that clients are able to choose.

I think it is important to add that all models can benefit from each other and that parts of each model may well be used in the other models. So, for example, the miracle question (solution-focused model) may be used within a narrative of transformative model, or even within the problem solving model. The technique of brainstorming about options (problem solving model) could be used within the solution-focused model.

Research of more than 40 years in psychotherapy showed that models are more alike then different. Therapies work not because of their unique explanatory schemes, specialized language, or specific techniques. On the contrary, their success is largely based on what they have in common (Bergin & Garfield, 1994). While the content of the techniques is different depending on the therapist's theoretical orientation, most procedures have the common quality of preparing clients to take some action to help themselves. Across all models, therapists expect their clients to do something different. In spite of all of the attention given to techniques and models in professional discourse, however, research indicates that they contribute a mere 15% to treatment outcome (Miller et al., 1997). Research shows that models significantly affect the behavior of therapists. However, client characteristics that were the same across treatment conditions predicted treatment outcome. *Clients, not therapists, make treatment work!* The same is probably true for mediators and the techniques and models they use.

Problem Solving Mediation and Solution-Focused Mediation: A Comparison

The problem solving model has originated from the cause-and-effect medical model (D'Zurilla & Goldfried, 1971) and consists of a number of established phases: the preparation and opening phase; the exploration phase: data collection, description by the clients of the conflict, and analysis of the conflict by the mediator; the motion and classification phase: searching for mutual interests; the negotiation phase: generating options and their subsequent implementation; and the rounding off phase: evaluation and closure.

This model is used in the Harvard Negotiating Project (Fisher & Ury, 1981). This model suggests that mediation is a process of identifiable phases and that the role of the mediator is to manage other people's negotiations. The goal is an agreement negotiated by the clients that satisfies the needs of all involved. Mediation is thus an exercise in problem solving. Deutsch and Coleman (2000) state that mediators need to remain process focused rather than outcome focused. They adhere to the problem solving model. In the solution-focused model the mediator tends to steer the process: Through asking questions he encourages the clients to look ahead to their preferred future and to how they can achieve this. Solution-focused mediation does not revolve around the outcome that the mediator deems appropriate, but around the outcome that the clients want to achieve.

Similarities. When in the problem solving model there is talk of *interests* and *options*, this model becomes more future oriented. Looking for the mutual interests in the motion and classification phase may contribute to defining the mutual goal. However, the goal of the positive outcome, has not yet been formulated. Generating options in the negotiation phase can define the means to realizing the mutual goal, but this is not a description of the desired outcome itself. Also, in the problem solving model, evaluation takes place: Did the changes in conduct lead to a positive outcome? However, in this model, it is not until the end of the mediation that changes are being evaluated; in the solution-focused model, each session includes an evaluation of what is better, scaling how close clients are to their mutual goal, and whether the session has been worth while and helpful.

Differences. In solution-focused mediation, conversations become solution-focused conversations as rapidly as possible, aimed at the preferred future of the clients involved. Conversations about the clients' *positions* and a familiarization with the history of the conflict are both deemed not only unneeded but also undesired, because of their negative influence on the atmosphere during the conversation and the unnecessary prolongation of the mediation. Attention is not so much paid to positions and to what clients do not want, but to the desired outcome and to what clients do want: the future with a difference. Solution-focused mediators ask, "What would you prefer instead of the conflict?" defined in positive, realistic, and concrete terms.

Talking about the past is not mediation since it is either judgment, trying to decide who is right and wrong from the past, or therapy, helping clients understand their past. In mediation, the concern about the past changes as a result of creating a different future, rather than reaching an understanding of the past (Haynes, Haynes, and Fong, 2004, p. 7).

De Bono (1985, p. 115) points out, "Management and problem solving are maintenance functions. They are not sufficient in a changing or a competitive world. Conceptual thinking is needed in addition." The solution-focused mediator is not only trained to assess the motivation of the client, but to relate to this and stimulate change. The steps considered crucial in problem-focused mediation – rom positions via interests to options – are in solution-focused mediation replaced by the steps of clients formulating a vision of their preferred future and solutions for achieving this goal.

Transformative Mediation and Solution-Focused Mediation: A Comparison

The transformative model of mediation regards conflict as a crisis of interaction and mediation as a process of conflict transformation. The role of the mediator is supporting the change in *empowerment* (personal growth from weakness to strength) and *recognition* (from self-interest to compassion and openness). As a result, the interaction between clients may change from destructive to constructive (Baruch et al., 2005).

Similarities. Control to a large extent remains in the hands of the clients, the mediator facilitates. One does not depart from the deficit model of the client, but from the competence model: Empowerment or autonomy is considered important in both transformative and solution-focused mediation. The importance of language is emphasized in directing the mediation, highlighting what clients are capable of and stressing their central role in the mediation. In the transformative model the past may be recalled in order to evoke a more positive image of the relationship as it used to be. In both forms of mediation the question relating to exceptions is asked: "When in the past did you manage to work together? How was this achieved?"

Differences. In solution-focused mediation, recognition is not a necessary ingredient, neither is there need for an explanation of the clients' positions. The focus on empowerment and recognition in the transformative model may be a part of the preferred future, but it is not the desired outcome itself. In the transformative model the mediation is considered a success when empowerment and recognition occur. Should the conflict then also be solved, this is seen as a welcome bonus, but it is not a necessity. Solution-focused mediation is directed at the preferred future of the clients, whatever that may be, and considers empowerment and recognition as a means to reaching that goal, and in that sense as a welcome bonus. In the transformative model, discussing the conflict and expressing emotions are considered essential. In the solution-focused model, the emotional impact of the conflict is acknowledged and validated; but discussing the conflict and expressing emotions are restricted as much as possible (see Chapter 10). Solution-focused mediation is not about feelings and emotions, but about cognitions and behavior, essentially what clients will be thinking and doing differently once they have reached their desired outcome.

Narrative Mediation and Solution-Focused Mediation: A Comparison

The narrative model is based upon the narrative therapy model according to White and Epston (1990). Winslade and Monk (2000) state that the emphasis in the narrative model is not so much on solving the conflict as the mediation's goal but rather on developing an *alternative story* of cooperation, understanding, and mutual respect. Together with the clients, the story behind the conflict is examined, revealing what negative effects this story has on the clients and on their relationship. The mediator looks for stories in the past that lie outside the conflict story (*unique outcomes*). With these elements, an alternative story is then constructed. A solution to the conflict is only one option in a long-term cooperation story. Mediation is considered a success when the participants know how they can continue their relationship. The task of the mediator is to give nuance to the stories and to bring the alternative story to light.

Similarities. The focus lies on possibilities. There exist no definitive explanations or descriptions of reality: *Social constructionism* (Cantwell & Holmes, 1994) is at the base of both narrative and solution-focused model. Language is seen as a form of social action and mediation is a place were clients and the mediator talk about the kind of world they are creating. The past is questioned to find the extent of past cooperation and to reveal a positive story. Both models aim at rewriting life stories and changing problem or conflict beliefs into solution-focused ideas. The focus is on what has worked (or is still working) rather than on what has not worked (or is not working). The focus has also changed from feeling to acting. Both models may use interventions aimed at *externalizing the conflict*: The conflict is detached; making it something that lies outside the clients and that has a negative influence on them. The conflict is regarded as the enemy by both the mediator and the clients, against which they can fight together (see Chapter 10). Both models use open questions ("what-," "when-," and "how-" questions) instead of closed questions. Problem-focused questions are changed into solution-focused questions: Language is important; it should be as mutual, respectful, and nonthreatening as possible.

Differences. Narrative mediation gives much more room to the history of the conflict. Much time is spent on deconstructing the conflict-saturated story of the clients. They are given the opportunity to cite when the conflict is especially apparent and in what way they then react. Goal formulation is less important and solving the conflict is only one of the options. In narrative mediation, by definition, the focus is on restoring a long-term cooperative relationship between clients. Less attention is paid to assessing and increasing the motivation of clients. The focus is on unique outcomes, almost the same as the focus on exceptions in the positive model. The difference is that exceptions are not unique and can be repeated, whereas unique outcomes cannot. With clients who see a solution-focused approach as too positive, who cannot find any exceptions for the conflict, and who cannot envisage a positive future, the narrative model might be a good alternative.

Conclusion

As described in Chapter 4, there are three main differences between traditional and solution-focused mediation:

- The *focus* of the mediation: In solution-focused mediation, the focus is on what clients want instead of the conflict, their preferred future.
- The development of solutions is not necessarily related to the conflict. Therefore, an *analysis of the conflict* itself is not useful in finding solutions.
- The *attitude of the mediator*: In solution-focused mediation the attitude of the mediator is not-knowing and leading from one step behind.

If the problem solving, the transformative, or the narrative model of mediation had been applied in the family case of the father and son described in Chapter 12, the mediation would have looked different. The mediator would have dealt with the past and present of the conflict at length. He would have taken an interest in exploring and analyzing the conflict and possibly a joint problem definition or explanatory hypothesis would have been developed. It would have been difficult to give the clients compliments and emphasize their competence if the conversations had focused on conflicts and failures: In problem solving mediation, earlier successes are not searched for. Only in solution-focused mediation does the desired outcome feature already at the beginning of the conversation: What are the father and son hoping for and what difference would that make to them, what is already working in the right direction, and which further steps can they take to reach their goal? Exploring and analyzing the conflicts past and present is not considered of importance for this.

In the three aforementioned models, the goal is not clearly described, neither do the clients determine it. These models are about conflict settlement or conflict resolution. Solution-focused mediation is about *conflict transformation*: What do clients want instead of the conflict? The importance of setting "stretch goals" is already described in Hope Theory (Chapter 2). "Stretch goals," goals that are difficult enough to be challenging, but easy enough to be accomplished, encourage the clients not only to resolve their conflicts, but also to move toward a more positive, strength-based stance.

Cloke (2006) also states that clients have a choice between merely settling conflicts and seeking to learn from them, correcting behaviors, and moving toward forgiveness and reconciliation. Questions concerning exceptions (see: unique outcomes) are also posed in the narrative model. Scaling questions are not used in the other three models. In the transformative model, the mediator would give plenty of room for the expression of emotions. Experience shows that clients sometimes stop the mediation because they see it as a repetition of the conflict, only this time at the table of the mediator: They lose hope for a future with a difference. In addition, from the start of mediation there often exists a complainant relationship between the clients and the mediator. In the three aforementioned models, there is little or no interest in increasing the motivation, resulting in the continuation of a complainant relationship, where clients do not see themselves as part of the conflict or part of the solutions. An evaluation of the mediation may have occurred at the end of the mediation and not, as in solution-focused mediation, by asking questions about progress ("What is better?"), scaling questions, and using the Session Rating Scale, as described in Chapter 12.

Research on Feedback

During the 1950s and 1960s a series of intriguing experiments were conducted on the nature and effect of feedback on human activity. In one study, two participants were exposed to a series of pictures of either healthy or sick cells (Watzlawick, 1976). Neither person in this study could actually see the other and each was given the assignment to learn to distinguish between the two types of cells through a process of trial and error. Small lights marked "right" or "wrong" were the source of feedback they received about their choices.

There was just one wrinkle in the experiment, of which both participants were unaware. Only one of them received accurate feedback about their guesses. When the light indicated he had made the right choice, he had indeed guessed correctly. On the other hand, feedback for the second participant was not based on his own, but rather on the guesses made by the first participant. Regardless of his choices, in other words, this person was told he was right if the other person had guessed correctly and wrong if the other had been incorrect. Data collected without their knowledge showed, at the conclusion of the experiment, that the first participant had learned to distinguish healthy from sick cells with an 80% rate of accuracy while the second continued to guess at no better than a chance rate.

The two types of feedback also had a distinct and interesting impact on the *theories* each participant developed over the course of the study to differentiate between healthy and sick cells. The participant who received accurate (reliable) feedback ended the experiment with a very simple, concrete, and parsimonious explanation. The second participant however, developed a complicated, subtle, and elaborate theory. This person, it must be recalled, had no way of knowing the feedback he received was not contingent on his own responses. Sometimes his responses happened to coincide with the correct answer, sometimes not. Given the inconsistent (unreliable) feedback, this participant was prevented from learning anything about his own actions and choices.

Even these results may not seem all that surprising. Something more troubling occurred when the two participants shared their respective theories with each other. In contrast to what one might hope and expect, the first participant was actually impressed with the complicated, mysterious, and ultimately unreliable theoretical formulations of his co-participant. The second, on the other hand, dismissed the statistically accurate theory of the first as "naïve and simplistic." In subsequent retests during which both participants received accurate feedback about their own guesses, the second continued to guess at little better than a chance rate. The performance of the first participant, however, who was now attempting to put some of the "brilliant" insights of their coparticipant into practice, significantly worsened.

The parallels between the results of this study and the field of mediation are striking. Historically divorced from systematic, reliable, and valid feedback about the outcome of mediation practices, the field has become a jumble of competing, complicated, and sometimes contradictory theories.

15 Personal Injury Mediation

Has anyone gone to war without seeing his own cause as just?
Justice does not bring peace, but is a major source of war
Erasmus

Case

Driving to work one morning, Ben (age 44), while waiting at a traffic light, is hit from behind by a van. The collision turns out to be not too serious, with only damage to the back of the car. The driver of the van apologizes and the accident claim forms are completed. However, after a few days Ben begins to experience neck pain. The pain increases, he is unable to continue his job as a construction worker and remains at home. Whiplash is the diagnosis of the family doctor.

Two months later Ben is still unable to work: His condition has not improved. He is considering making a compensation claim and on more than one occasion, he calls the van driver's insurance company, with discussions becoming increasingly heated. Because of the lack of progress, he decides to engage a lawyer to act on his behalf. The conflict escalates: The insurance company states that the seriousness of the whiplash injury cannot be solely the result of a small collision and that the complaints are probably mostly psychological. A connection with problems at work at the time of the collision is suggested. Finally, the insurance company offers a settlement of $10,000.

Ben and his lawyer do not accept this proposal, which in their view is much too low – Ben is at risk of losing his job – and initiate legal proceedings against the insurance company. The company responds by requesting an independent report from both an orthopedic specialist and a psychiatrist. Ben reacts furiously to the suggestion that he has psychological problems and later, following an emotional confrontation in court, the judge proposes mediation. After some hesitation the parties concerned agree to this.

Seven months after the collision, the first meeting takes place. Present are Ben, his lawyer, a representative of the insurance company named

Fred, and a company lawyer. The mediator welcomes everyone and gives an explanation of the solution-focused mediation procedure. The focus in the conversations will be on what those concerned would like instead of the conflict and how they can achieve this, rather than on the conflict itself and what has preceded this.

The mediator also gives compliments for the willingness to sit at the table of the mediator: All appear motivated to resolve this case through mediation. The mediator gives Ben and Fred, should they wish to, the opportunity to briefly express their emotions; they get one chance to "say what definitely needs to be said." Ben seizes this opportunity to vent his anger about the slow progress and the demands made by the insurance company. The mediator gives recognition to Ben's anger and concerns: They are understandable. Fred indicates that he would like to resolve the case fairly. In addition, he says that he can understand that Ben is worried about his future. This remark lessens the tension in the room.

The mediator then changes the seating arrangement: Ben and Fred are asked to take another position at the mediator's table, from sitting next to each other and not talking directly to each other they are invited to sit in a 90 degree angle. The lawyers are asked to sit back and just listen to what their clients are saying. They are invited to give their comments at a later point in the meeting. The mediator asks what they are hoping for and what difference that would make (goal formulation). Ben is hoping for a quick conclusion. He is not willing to cooperate with respect to the proposed medical examinations; the necessity for a psychiatric report he finds particularly ridiculous. The difference for him would be that he would no longer need to feel insecure about the outcome of this lengthy case and that he could put all this in the past. He feels angry and is not sleeping well. He is also worried about his health and about keeping his job. The mediator asks what he would like to see instead of the worry and anger if his hope were to become reality. Ben states that he would then sleep well again and his mood would improve. Furthermore, he would feel confident that he could continue with his life.

Fred says that he has no desire to prolong the case, he too is hoping for a quick settlement. For him, the difference would be that he would be free of this emotional man and that he would feel like he has settled the case in a decent and proper manner.

After this, the mediator asks what is already going in the right direction to achieve their goal. It appears that Ben is surprised about the insurance company's willingness to engage in mediation, apparently he had not expected that. Also helpful is the fact that at the table they talk more calmly than they did on the telephone. Fred's sympathetic remark is also constructive. Moreover, the presence and support of both lawyers, specialized in physical injuries, is considered by both clients to be beneficial.

Again, the mediator gives compliments for the steps that have already been taken in the right direction.

The mediator asks a scaling question, "If a 10 is *pure cooperation* and a 0 is *pure conflict*, where would both say they are right now?" Ben answers with a 3 and Fred with a 4. At the end of the first meeting, the mediator asks Ben and Fred if they would find a return visit useful. Both agree and schedule another appointment. The mediator then ends the meeting with the request that, in the meantime, both reflect on what could be the next step. Which step can they take themselves and which step would they like to see the other person take? They will discuss this with their lawyers in the intervening period and focus on this in the next meeting.

At the request of Ben and Fred, the second meeting, which turns out to be the final one, takes place three weeks later. Both lawyers are again present. The mediator opens the conversation with a question relating to what is better. In the past weeks, Ben has begun to feel somewhat better, his anger has diminished to some extent. However, the neck pain persists. Fred is pleased that the first meeting put both on speaking terms: The air has cleared somewhat. This is also evident from the fact that Ben and Fred begin the session with a handshake. The mediator compliments both on this progress.

As a proposal for the next step, the lawyer of the insurance company offers an amount of $25,000. As a next step, Ben and his lawyer see compensation of $50,000 to be acceptable. After some negotiating the lawyers arrive at an amount of $40,000, payable within a month as compensation for material damages and loss of working ability. This is included in the settlement agreement, which is signed at the end of the meeting. Ben is visibly relieved that the case has ended. He says that he is now able to continue with his life. Fred is satisfied: He feels that the case has been resolved fairly. There are also positive reactions from the lawyers, who for the first time were present at mediation; they had not expected to be able to achieve a satisfying result so quickly. The mediator gives compliments to all for their efforts and motivation to reach a solution together. The mediation is concluded.

Since this mediation took place, the insurance company decided to change their policy and invite people for a face-to-face conversation instead of trying to solve disputes on the phone.

Seating Arrangements

Topographic interventions are interventions in which the mediator is the director who gives suggestions to the clients as where to sit at the mediator's table. They require that the mediator does not see the seating arrangement as coincidental and unimportant, but wonders whether the seat each person takes, is functional for the mediation process. Erickson, mentioned in Chapter 3, often used topographic interventions. For example, he asked a child to leave the room for a while, so his mother could take his place: when the mother took the seat of her child, she could think more clearly about him and his point of view.

Also the mediator should not be too strongly tied to a seat. When supportive, the mediator can move their chair a bit closer to the client. By sliding their chair a bit backwards, they can indicate that they do not want to participate in the conversation (see Chapter 10: Interventions for Clients Who Argue). Each seating arrangement has its own effect. The way in which the clients are seated in relation to each other and the mediator is a major structural intervention: It makes, in a nonverbal way, clear what is expected of the clients and how they are supposed to behave in front of each other and the mediator. It can stress the status and authority of the mediator and the way communication is supposed to happen.

Possible seating arrangements are:

- No table and seats relatively close to each other: informal;
- Round table or trapezoidal table: equality;
- Clients sit in a 90-degree angle and relatively close to each other: cooperation;
- Clients sit opposite each other: danger of escalation, but also encouragement to talk to each other because they look at each other;
- Clients sit next to each other and face the mediator: the mediator is the expert, but this does not encourage clients to talk to each other;
- Big (oval) table: clients sit at the head: creates safety in emotional conflicts.

The mediator may change the seating arrangements at the beginning or during the meeting or can invite clients to go to a different room altogether. Selekman, a well-known psychotherapist, has two rooms: a problem-focused room and a solution-focused room. "Sometimes we go into a completely different room when beginning this part of the assessment session." I say, "Now we can talk about solutions and change – where you want to be when we have a successful outcome here" (1997, p. 57). Not every mediator will be so fortunate as to have a problem room and a solutions room and that is not necessary, of course.

Case

Mr. and Mrs. Jones sit at the mediator's table because they are divorcing. The atmosphere is grim; they do not look at each other. They have not spoken to each other for several months. Both clients sit next to each other at the table, opposite the mediator and so the conversation is directed only at the mediator and not at each other. After they have had the chance to say what they definitely would like to say and have given a summary of the events leading to their divorce, the mediator asks them to change their seats and sit in an angle of 90 degrees. The mediator explains briefly what the reason is for this change: The conversation will now be about their cooperation as parents of their children in the future.

Somewhat surprised, the clients do what the mediator has asked them. It then becomes easier for the clients to look at each other – although very shortly – and design their cooperation in the future. Moreover, the mediator is no longer the center of the conversation.

Dollars and Cents

Solution-focused conflict management can be effective in domestic situations, contract negotiations, and even in criminal mediations. In these scenarios, non-traditional agreements are more easily developed. These situations are usually accompanied by a great deal of emotion from the clients involved.

As a result, words of validation and apologies may carry significant weight. Foa and Foa (1975) developed a theory about the kinds of compensation that are considered appropriate as repayment for certain kinds of concessions. They identify two dimensions: concreteness (tangibility) and particularism (the extent to which the value of the resource depends on the identity of the person who delivers it). Love and status are particularistic resources; goods and money are nonparticularistic resources. In their studies, they showed that a form of compensation is more appropriate, the closer it is to the resource received. Thus, goods can properly be exchanged for money and status for love. But money cannot properly be exchanged for love or a good relationship. Therefore, powerful tools for improving or ending a relationship in the best possible way can be a personal meeting with mutual acknowledgment and understanding or one in which apologies are offered.

Solution-focused conflict management may be fertile ground for finding creative solutions because the issues at hand are more complex than just simple dollar figures. Clients can be helped to realize that no conflict is as simply defined as a matter of dollars and cents.

16 Failures

When you discover you are riding a dead horse, the best strategy
is to dismount
Dakota Indians

Failures

In solution-focused conflict management, failures often involve a breakdown of negotiation involving an answer to the question, "How will you know when we can stop meeting like this?" (De Shazer, 1994). The clients are willing to accept the absence of the conflict as a good enough goal, but the absence of the conflict can never be proved and, therefore, neither clients nor mediator can know success or failure. Unless clearly established beforehand, even the presence of positive changes is not enough to prove the absence of the conflict. Therefore questions like, "What are your best hopes?" and "What difference would that make?" are considered essential for establishing a well defined goal in conflict management.

Some failures can be seen as related to a difficulty in shifting from a conflict-focused conversation into a solution-focused conversation. The fault here is situated neither on the mediator's side nor on the client's side: both are in it together. Most frequently the mediator has been unable to help the clients see exceptions to the conflict as differences that can be made to make a difference and thus as precursors of the goal of the clients.

■ Exercise 17

Ask your clients, "How will you know you do not have to come here anymore?" or "How will we know we can stop meeting like this?" Then, as a follow-up question, ask, "How confident are you that you are on track to getting what you want?" The responses to these questions will give you some hints about your next step. Are the clients saying they are on track? What else do they need?

Pathways to Impossibility

Duncan et al. (1997) describe four *pathways to impossibility*. The first pathway arises in the *anticipation of impossibility*. Historically, impossibility has been located in the client. In a well-known experiment, Rosenhan (1973) recruited and trained a group of normal confederates (one of them was Martin Seligman, founder of the *positive psychology*, see Chapter 1) to obtain psychiatric hospitalization. To gain admission, they falsified a single psychotic symptom (hearing voices). The clinicians diagnosed the pretend patients as mentally ill and admitted them for stays ranging from 7 to 52 days. During their hospitalizations, the pseudopatients showed no signs of psychosis, yet the original diagnosis remained in place. Rosenhan also demonstrated how the clinician's initial expectations came to serve as confirmatory biases. In one instance, staff took truthful historical information provided by a pseudopatient and made it conform to prevailing theoretical notions about schizophrenia. Therefore, the mediator's expectation of impossibility will probably distort new information to conform to his expectations.

The second pathway to impossibility is the *professional's traditions or conventions*. Mediators are often eager to corroborate their theory with each client. Their theory is often overapplied and the benefits of allegiance are overstated. Remember the story of the man who bought a hammer and then found that everything needed to be nailed. Clients have their own theories about their lives and their problems and when their points of view are ignored or dismissed by the mediator's theory, noncompliance or resistance is a predictable outcome. To the mediator, the client begins to look, feel, and act impossible; to the client, the mediator comes across as uncaring or disinterested. The mediation changes from a helping relationship to a clash of cultures with no one the winner. In Chapter 12, client-directed, outcome-informed mediation is described as an answer to this second pathway to impossibility.

The third pathway to impossibility is persisting in *an approach that is not working*. Watzlawick et al. (1974) reasoned that unmanageable problems, those that are often called chronic, couldn't be sufficiently explained on the basis of innate characteristics of the client. Rather, they concluded that the unyielding or impossible nature of a problem arises in the very efforts to solve it. For a difficulty to turn into a problem, only two conditions need to be fulfilled. First, the difficulty is mishandled; the attempted solution does not work. And second, when the difficulty proves refractory, more of the same ineffective solution is applied and the original difficulties will deteriorate. Over time, a vicious downward spiraling cycle ensues with the original difficulty growing into an impasse, immense in size and importance.

Mediators doing more of the same are sometimes convinced that persistence will eventually win the day, even when all the evidence suggests that the strategy is ineffectual. All theoretical models and strategies are inherently limited and will generate their share of impossibility when repetitively applied. Some research done in psychotherapy shows the following. The same might be true for mediation.

Wampold (2001) found that when there is no improvement after the third session, chances are 75% that the therapy will fail. This percentage is 90% when no improvement is found after the sixth session.

Research by Lambert et al. (1996) indicate that treatment should be brief when little or no progress is being made in the early sessions: Then, it should be as short in duration as possible. As long as clients are making document-able progress and are interesting in continuing, however, treatment should be extended.

The fourth and last pathway to impossibility is created when that mediator *neglects the client's motivation*. There is no such individual as an unmotivated client. Clients may not share the ideas and goal of the mediator, but they hold strong motivations of their own. An unproductive mediation can come about by mistaking or overlooking what the clients want to accomplish, misapprehending the client's readiness for change, or pursuing a personal motivation. Research has established that the critical process-outcome in psychotherapy is the quality of the client's participation in a positive working alliance (see Chapter 8). The motivation of the clients not only for sitting at the mediator's table, but also for achieving their own goal, has to be understood, respected, and actively incorpo-rated into the mediaton. To do less or to impose agendas motivated by theoreti-cal prerogatives, personal bias, and perhaps some sense of what would be good for the clients, invites impossibility.

Research (Piper et al., 1999) showed that dropouts could be predicted by treatment process variables, not by client variables. In other words, only what happened in the sessions predicted whether the client failed to return, not who the client was and what the client brought to the process.

Case

Ms. A (employer) and Mr. B (employee) are at the table of the mediator. Mr. B says, "I do not think that this mediation will succeed; the former mediator has also not helped us much. We did make an agreement, but the implementation of what was agreed has never come off the ground. It has only led to more arguments and on top of that I cannot work any-more." The (overoptimistic) mediator ignores this remark (even though Mr. B repeats that it should be up to the judge to take a decision) and before long the mediation reaches a deadlock. The mediator would have done better to validate the doubts of Mr. B by asking scaling questions with respect to his confidence and hope. Then there would have been an opening to increase his confidence and hope. "Suppose you would have a bit more hope, what difference would that make?" Also, the mediator could have asked, "How, despite your earlier experience, do you manage to sit here at the table?"

Solution-Focused Questions in Case of Failure

Top performers review the details of their performance, identifying specific actions and alternate strategies for reaching their goals. Where unsuccessful learners arrtibute failure to external and uncontrollable factors ("I had a bad day"), experts know exactly what they do and more often cite controllable factors ("I should have done this instead of that"). Average professionals are far likelier to spend time hypothesizing about failed strategies – believing perhaps that understanding the reasons why an approach did not work will lead to better outcomes – and less time thinking about strategies that might be more effective.

Walter and Peller (1992) give some advice on what to do in situations where there seems to be no progress. Ask yourself as a mediator these questions:

- Who is the client (who wants to change)?
- What is the client's goal?
- Do you have a goal and not a wish? Is the goal well defined and within the control of the clients?
- Are you and the clients looking for too much too fast? Try looking for smaller change.
- Do clients not do tasks you have been expecting them to do? You can provide some feedback to think about rather than an action-oriented task.
- If you have gone through all the above steps, is there anything you need to do differently? Sometimes we are too close to the trees to see the forest and may not recognize a nonproductive pattern between the clients and us. A team or consultant may be helpful to provide a more detached frame of reference.

Saving Face

The place of *saving face* should be considered. When clients feel overwhelmed and stuck, they are apt to experience their problems as impossible. Seeking help offers the prospect of something better. Simultaneously, it may also signify their failure ro resolve the problem on their own. In fact, their feelings of failure may be so acute that they crowd out any favorable self-evaluation. In these circumstances, going to therapy can represent just one more unpleasant reminder of how badly they have managed their difficulties. Humiliation is added to insult. If a therapist then suggests or implies that the client's point of view is wrong, somehow invalidate, or upstage the client, resistance may appear. After all, even if not already demoralized, who wants to be reminded of failure, critized, judged or made to feel that you have to follow orders? What we come to call resistance may sometimes reflect the client's attempt to salvage a small portion or self-respect. As such, some cases become impossible simply because the treatment allows the client no way of saving face or upholding dignity. This is probably what Erickson had in mind when he suggested that the art of therapy revolves around helping clients to bow out of their symptoms gracefully. He recognized that clients simultaneously hold a desire to change and a natural tendency to protect themselves if change (for worse or for better) compromises personal dignity (Duncan et al., 1997, p. 12).

17 Victim-Offender Mediation

*Justice leading to reconciliation is a better path than justice
in the form of retaliation*
Desmond Tutu

Restorative Justice

This chapter discusses the development and characteristics of restorative justice, through the example of the South African Truth and Reconciliation Commission (TRC). It will compare this conciliatory model with mediation and briefly discuss its implications for this discipline.

In many countries, imprisonment is society's most drastic measure for dealing with offenders. In essence, punitive measures are a response to impermissible actions in the form of *retaliation*: the intentional infliction of suffering through detention. Different perceptions underlie the criminal justice system. For example, according to the philosopher Immanuel Kant, retaliation is an appropriate response, stemming from the moral duty to give perpetrators their just deserts. Another view places the *usefulness* of the punishment centrally, for both perpetrator and society. This view also encompasses the aspect of re-socialization: During his detention the perpetrator is encouraged to change his conduct and attitude.

Both of these perspectives on criminal justice are perpetrator-oriented. On behalf of society (including the victim), a certain punishment is imposed on the person found guilty. In this process, the perpetrator is passive: He is often represented by an attorney and is usually advised to plead not guilty.

However, many victims gain no satisfaction from this procedure. For the victim to come to terms with and recover from what happened to them, it is often important that they are given the opportunity to express themself face to face with the wrongdoer, that their questions are answered, and that their suffering is recognized as a result of the perpetrator taking responsibility for their actions, admitting guilt, and, preferably, also apologizing (Bannink 2006a, 2008a, 2008b, 2008c, 2008d).

Through the last years, *restorative justice* has added to these traditional views on criminal justice. Within this form of justice, it is not the wrongdoer but the victim who takes centre stage. Zehr (2002) suggests the following definition, "Restorative justice is a process to involve, to the extent possible, those who have a stake in a specific offense and to collectively identify and address harms, needs and obligations, in order to heal and put things as right as possible."

Restorative justice is not aimed at criminal sanctions, but at repairing damage or suffering that has been inflicted on the victim or on society. It focuses on the reintegration of both victim and perpetrator, for example through *restorative mediation*, which brings victim and offender together in a safe and structured context. When the defendant is prepared to take some responsibility for their actions and admit guilt, restorative mediation should be possible in every phase of the criminal procedure.

Reconciliation

The Boer War in South Africa (1899–1902) was concluded with the signing of the *Peace of Vereeniging*, including amnesty with regard to war crimes. However, the amnesty led to suspicion, bitterness, and hatred because it turned out to be a peace without justice. The war had caused disruption, trauma, and impoverishment among South Africans, forcing them to find work in the cities, where they were dominated by whites and failed to gain the rights they felt they were entitled to. This resulted in clashes, which would lead, in 1948, to the institution of the Apartheid regime.

After the abolishment of Apartheid, it was understood (as a result of the experience gained following the Boer War) that a violent conflict couldn't be satisfactorily ended solely with a peace treaty and a general amnesty. Rather, on the cessation of hostilities, the trauma experienced by those involved should be addressed as quickly as possible. This prompted the government to institute the Truth and Reconciliation Commission or TRC in 1995 – a commission inquiring into all apartheid-related crimes – chaired by Archbishop Desmond Tutu. The installation of the TRC was a political compromise agreed to by most parties. Anybody who felt they had been the victim of violence could come forward and be heard at the TRC. Perpetrators of violence could also give testimony and request amnesty from prosecution.

Central to the TRC's method was the granting of amnesty in exchange for the truth. Individual amnesties were only given to perpetrators who revealed, in full, the facts regarding their involvement in the crimes during the Apartheid regime. Furthermore, these crimes had to have been politically motivated. The mandate of the TRC was to bear witness to, record, and, in some cases, grant amnesty to the perpetrators of crimes relating to human rights violations, facilitate reparation, and rehabilitation. The latter was addressed by giving victims the opportunity to relate their experiences and by suggesting reparations as compensation for past and present wrongs. Around 22,000 victims sent in petitions; around 2,000 people were finally allowed to tell their story in public. Among the perpetrators, there were 7,000 petitioners, of whom 1,200 were granted amnesty. The TRC was seen by many as a crucial component of the transition to full and free democracy in South Africa and is generally regarded as successful.

Yet the conciliatory model of the commission has also been criticized. A central objection to the commission's endeavors related to the token cooperation demonstrated by the white community; government leaders such as Pieter Willem Botha refused to come forward and give testimony. In addition, the forced nature of the process could convey a distorted image of reconciliation: To what extent was the reconciliation imposed, and thus not sincere? The commission was bestowed with the authority to hear and try cases and make legal decisions, which were, however, not verified in a court of law. Moreover, the granting of amnesty to wrongdoers deprived the victims of the opportunity to see justice done.

Steve Biko was killed under the apartheid regime. His son describes the commission's interrogation of five defendants, "It was the first time that I was able to look my father's murderers in the eye. I experienced a whole range of emotions, but I refused to let myself fall into the traps laid by these people." Even though amnesty was refused, the process disappointed Biko. "Nobody stood up to tell the truth or apologize. All five defendants related a different story. In our case, the TRC has clearly failed to reveal the truth." He spoke these words before it was announced that the case would not be taken to court due to a lack of evidence.

In spite of all this, he praises the commission's efforts. "It has ensured that relative calm prevails in our country, avoiding the possibility of witch-hunts. And for many South Africans, it was an eye-opener to be confronted with the crimes that in fact took place right under their noses."

This process has also led to recognition of the potential and limits of reconciliation: Many South Africans now understand that reconciliation is a long-term process with an indefinite end point. They realize that it is more concerned with the everyday reality of learning to live together than with single encounters at forums such as the TRC.

There are similarities and differences with regular mediation. In his article *Bemiddeling deur waarheid na versoening: die slothoofdstuk op die traumatische nalatenskap van die Suid-Afrikaanse geskiedenis?*, De Bruin (2008) outlines some similarities between the TRC and mediation, which he calls *mediated settlement*:

- The TRC is the mediator between two formerly opposing parties.
- The TRC is not a court of law but a quasi-judicial body.
- The mediators of the TRC were impartial, trained, and deemed fit for the task.
- One of the (secondary) goals of the TRC was to facilitate communication between the participants, so that discord and accusations would not increase, but rather reconciliation could take place. The primary goal was to ensure that South African society would be stable and peaceful. In this process, the formal recognition of the violation of the rights of the victims was seen as the first step towards reconciliation.

De Bruin also mentions several *differences* compared with mediation:

- The TRC was bestowed with the authority to force perpetrators to be present in a mediation process and indicate for what reason they had violated the rights of individuals. Thus the accused were not always voluntarily present. Yet perpetrators were given every opportunity to voluntarily participate in the process.
- Because of the expansive nature of the commission, the mediators were not necessarily acceptable to all participants. The mediators were, however, chosen with great care to ensure as far as possible their impartiality.
- People who were not directly involved, for example, village leaders, could give testimonies.
- The TRC was bestowed with the authority to put forward recommendations to the government with regard to the reparation of the violated rights of the victims.
- The testimonies of the victims were made in public, as were the requests for amnesty by the perpetrators. Confidentiality, which in mediation is guaranteed, was not part of the process.

I may add to this list that a primary goal of the TRC was to reveal the truth. In mediation, this is not an absolute necessity. Another difference is that restorative justice, unlike mediation, provides a context and language for specifically naming and dealing with wrongdoing and injustice. It allows space for concepts of right and wrong, of justice and injustice, to be named and explored and provides a conflict-resolving concept of justice to facilitate that process.

De Bruin commented: "Peace without justice is only a short-term solution, like leaving a smoldering fire unattended. This is especially true if trauma is the main ingredient, likely to flare up again." The goal of all forms of restorative justice, including the Truth and Reconciliation Commission-model, is to bring participants into a reconciliation process with regard to their actions and the consequences thereof. This can be seen as a form of mediation, where not the sword but the word triumphs.

In case individual help in overcoming trauma is needed in addition, the solution-focused model in psychotherapy is a good choice, with an emphasis on posttraumatic success instead of posttraumatic stress (Bannink, 2007b, 2008d).

An important implication for mediation is that the end of the conflict alone is insufficient. If it concerns a long-term relationship between participants, one needs to take a step further in the form of *restoring the relationship* (reconciliation).

According to Archbishop Desmond Tutu, "Criminal procedures and police investigations are slow and inefficient. Confession, forgiveness and reconciliation in the lives of nations are not just airy-fairy religious and spiritual things, nebulous and unrealistic. They are the stuff of practical politics." The concept of a reconciliatory commission has been adopted in other countries, such as Nepal and Uganda, but unfortunately remains in the planning stage up until the present day.

Reconciliation is also observed in the animal kingdom. (De Waal, 2000). High-ranking primates sometimes adopt a control role, breaking up fights, or systematically protecting the weak against the strong. At other times, they intervene peacefully or try to calm down one of the participants. In species in which large males defend units of several females, such as Chinese golden monkeys, the leading male may maintain harmony by interposing himself between female contestants while holding their hands, and stroking or grooming both of them. In macaques and vervets, relatives of the victim may seek contact with the opponent. For example, a mother may approach and groom the attacker of her daughter in what appears a reconciliation on behalf of her offspring. Similarly, there exist field reports of intergroup reconciliations spearheaded by the alpha females of different monkey groups. In perhaps the most complex pattern, thus far known of chimpanzees only, a female acts as catalyst by bringing male rivals together. After a fight between them, males may remain oriented toward each other, staying close, but without either one initiating an actual reunion. Females have been observed to break the deadlock by grooming one male, then the other, until she has brought the two of them together, after which she withdraws. Research in such mammals as domestic goats, spotted hyenas, and bottlenose dolphins suggest that conflict resolution may be widespread indeed.

All of these tactics are elaborations on a basic behavioral mechanism that protects cooperative bonds. The evolutionary advantages of reconciliation are obvious for animals that survive thought mutual aid: reconciliation ensures the continuation of cooperation among parties with partially conflicting interests.

Victim-Offender Mediation

In 1974, the first case of what is called the Victim Offender Reconciliation Program took place in Ontario. Apart from *victim-offender mediation (VOM)* today other models are used in the restorative justice field. *Family group conferences (FGCs)* originated in New Zealand in 1989, responding to the concerns and values of the indigenous Maori tradition. These are facilitated encounters with a large circle of participants, including not only victims and offenders, but also family members, police, and others. In New Zealand, FGCs form the hub of the entire juvenile justice system, with courts serving as a backup instead of the norm (Zehr, 2004).

An even larger circle of participants is included in *peacemaking circles*. These circles usually include community members and are facilitated by a "circle keeper." Initially entering the restorative justice field from Canadian First Nation indigenous roots, circles have been widely adapted not only in cases involving crime, but also within schools, religious institutions, and the workplace.

There is some discomfort with the term mediation, because unlike civil mediations, there is often a clear case of wrongdoing in criminal cases, and victims are often uncomfortable with the moral neutrality implied by the term mediation.

Zehr (2004) hopes that ways can be found to address the following questions not only in restorative processes, but in conflict transformation processes as well:

- Who has been hurt in this situation, and what are their needs?
- What obligations result from these hurts and needs, and whose obligations are they?
- What are the causes of these hurts and needs, and what can be done to address them?
- Who has a stake in this situation?
- What is the appropriate process to involve these stakeholders in an effort to put things right and resolve the conflicts?

Victim-offender mediation programs bring together victims of crime and their convicted offenders for discussion with the assistance of trained mediators (also called facilitators). There is often the possibility of face-to-face dialogue between victims and offenders who want to participate. In case the victim has been killed, family members may choose to initiate the mediation process after the offender's trial and conviction. Offenders do not receive leniency or parole consideration for their participation in victim-offender mediation. Research on victim-offender mediation reports high levels of satisfaction for both victims and offenders who participated in both nonviolent and severely violent crimes (Umbreit, 2001).

Walker and Hayashi (2007) describe the history and the features of the Pono Kaulike program in Hawai. Pono Kaulike means, "equal rights and justice for all."

The program began in 2003 and is named after a resolution enacted by the Hawaii State judiciary in 2000, which states that the "Hawaii State Judiciary shall continue to act in accordance with the principles of Restorative Justice and the concept of Pono Kaulike..." The pilot program was conceived and provided by a small nonprofit organization that has assisted organizations in developing, implementing, and evaluating restorative justice programs since 1996. Pono Kaulike uses the solution-focused brief therapy approach, which carefully uses language, and appreciates the importance of relationships in assisting troubled people to find their own solutions to problems. Pono Kaulike evolved to provide three distinct types of restorative justice meetings: restorative conferences, restorative dialogs, and restorative sessions.

Restorative conferences are meetings that include the defendant, victim, and supporters of both parties. The group discusses how each party has been affected by the wrongdoing and how the harm may be repaired. A written agreement is developed that specifies what the defendant is to do to repair the harm done to victims. A restorative dialog occurs when the defendant and victim meet without the presence of family or friends. They enter into an agreement regarding the responses of each to the harm that has occurred. A restorative session occurs when the victim and/or the defendant and their supporters meet separately with facilitators. A "restorative plan" is developed to include self-improvement goals and victim-defendant reconciliation actions. The program's experiences have shown that the types of cases most appropriate for Pono Kaulike are those that involve parties with an ongoing relationship, such as relative, neighbors, friends, spouses, or those with an intimate relationship.

Research of the program's effectiveness demonstrated extremely high participant satisfaction, a decrease in recidivism in one important area, and agreement compliance, which included a higher level of restitution payments than what is normally obtained from court ordered restitution.

> The solution-focused approach fits naturally with restorative justice processes, because both address problem solving in positive ways that can increase individual and community self-efficacy and empowerment. Both the solution-focused approach and restorative justice generate optimism and hopefulness for the future, regardsless of the past. Optimism is vital for individuals to develop coping skills and resiliency. Restorative justice using the solution-focused approach are powerful processes that can build relationships and community out of wrongdoing (Walker et al., 2006, p. 4).

Most VOM models incorporate premediation work and (therapeutic) conversations with both victim and offender. Once the victim requests a dialogue with the offender, the offender is contacted and asked to participate.

Essential elements at the onset of the dialogue between victim and offender include topics like an introduction of names, the purpose of the meeting, procedures for the interaction, who will participate in the mediation session, procedures for taking a break, the mediator's role, ground rules, specific ground rules created by participants, and a question prompting participants if they are ready to begin the session.

The mediator explains that the mediation begins by having the victim provide an initial statement, and then the offender is asked to give an opening statement. The role of the mediator is mostly one of witness to the process. He may say, "I am just here to help both of you, to help to facilitate the dialogue between you. To help clarify questions, needs, issues of purpose that you may have. I am not here to impose my expectations or solutions: it is all yours." The mediator also offers encouragement to the participants, "I really want to tell you how much I appreciate the fact that you are here today talking to each other."

In their opening statements the victim and offender include their purpose for participating and what they want to accomplish (goal formulation).

Case

Mediator: Are you all ready? I'll go over some stuff with you. Like I said earlier, the preparation we have done for these months has now led us and given us the foundation for what we are about today. For you, Rachel (victim) to have the opportunity to meet with you, Bill (offender), to facilitate healing and recovery.

What we are about can be very personal and very emotional. We presume it is difficult, maybe painful. What we're doing today is based on creating a safe place built on trust and openness, honesty, sensitivity. Toward the end of establishing personal safety, what is done and said here is said in confidence. Each of you, all of us, have signed confidentiality forms, including the corrections officer outside. You are free to share and not share as you choose. I am just here to help you.

Our ground rules are: no name-calling and no obscenities or any kind of disruptive actions. When one of you is talking, don't interrupt the other. You both have paper and pen and you can jot things down, and you can remember to ask later.

Our time here, our time together, will be according to your own needs, your individual needs and your mutual needs. We will take breaks whenever necessary. If I don't take one soon enough, just let me know. As far as the dialogue itself, we will begin with Rachel. I will ask you to give a brief opening statement, just a couple of sentences. And then I will ask the same of you, Bill. Then, we will go back to Rachel and she will start the actual dialogue between you. At the conclusion of the dialogue we have the option to develop together an affirmation agreement.

I want to affirm your commitment and trust in this process and also acknowledge both your hard work and willingness to be vulnerable today. Other than that, are you ready? Okay. Rachel if you want to go ahead and just give an opening statement on your purpose for being here and what you want to accomplish. (Szmania, 2006, p. 120).

Epilogue by Fredrike Bannink

A monk on his journey home comes to the banks of a wide river. Staring hopelessly at the great obstacle in front of him, he ponders for hours on just how to cross such a wide barrier. Just as he is to give up his journey, he sees a great Zen teacher on the other side of the river. The monk yells over to the teacher 'Oh Master, can you tell me how to get to the other side of this river?' The teacher ponders for a moment, looks up and down the river and yells back 'You are already on the other side.'

What does it take to become a solution-focused mediator? The answer of Steve de Shazer would be, "Only a small change is needed." And I think he is right. Because when you look at what you are already doing in the right direction, you will undoubtedly find many strengths, competencies, and resources that you already possess. From there on, you may design what the next (small) step might be or what you would consider to be the next significant sign of progress.

With solution-focused conflict management and an emphasis on client-directed and outcome-informed rules of play, a lot can change for the better for our clients, for ourselves, for our colleague mediators, and for the world. I hope reading this book has been one of those steps in the right direction. Maybe you are already on the other side.

Epilogue by Kenneth Cloke

Over the last three decades, hundreds of thousands of people around the world have been trained in community, divorce, family, commercial, organizational, and workplace mediation, as well as in allied conflict resolution skills such as collaborative negotiation, group facilitation, public dialogue, restorative justice, victim-offender mediation, ombudsmanship, collaborative law, consensus decision making, creative problem solving, prejudice reduction and bias awareness, conflict resolution systems design, and dozens of associated practices.

Among the most important and powerful of these skills are a number of core ideas and interventions that originate in psychology, particularly in what is commonly known as "brief therapy," where the border separating conflict resolution from psychological intervention has become indistinct, and in many places blurred beyond recognition. Examples of the positive consequences of blurring this line can be found inrecent discoveries in neurophysiology, "emotional intelligence," and solution-focused approaches to conflict resolution.

While it is, of course, both necessary and vital that we recognize the key differences between the professions of psychology and conflict resolution, it is *more* necessary and vital, especially in these times, that we recognize their essential similarities, collaborate in developing creative new techniques, and invite them to learn as much as they can from each other.

Beyond this, I believe it is increasingly important for us to *consciously* generate a fertile, collaborative space between them; discourage the tendency to jealously guard protected territory; and oppose efforts to create new forms of private property in techniques that reduce hostility and relieve suffering.

It is, therefore, critical that we think carefully and strategically about how best to translate a deeper understanding of the emotional and neurophysiological underpinnings of conflict and resolution processes into practical, hands-on mediation techniques; that we explore the evolving relationship between mediation and psychology, and other professions as well; and that we translate that understanding into improved ways ofhelping people become competent, successful mediators, as Fredrike Bannink sets out to do in the present volume.

Among the urgent reasons for doing so are the rise of increasingly destructive global conflicts that *cannot* be solved even by a single nation, let alone by a single style, approach, profession, or technique; the persistence of intractable conflicts that require more advanced techniques; and the recent rise of innovative, transformational techniques that form only a small part of the curriculum of most mediation trainings. [For more on mediating global conflicts, see my book, *Conflict Revolution: Mediating Evil, War, Injustice, and Terrorism – How Mediators Can Help Save the Planet,* Janis Publications 2008.]

The present generation is being asked a profound set of questions that require immediate action based on complex, diverse, complementary, even contradictory answers. In my judgment, thesequestions include:

- What is our responsibility as global citizens for solving the environmental, social, economic, and political conflicts that are taking place around us?
- Is it possible to successfully apply conflict resolution principles to the inequalities, inequities, and dysfunctions that are continuing to fuel chronic social, economic, and political conflicts?
- Can we find ways of working beyond national, religious, ethnic, and professional borders so as to strengthen our capacity for international collaboration and help save the planet?
- Can we build bridges across diverse disciplines so as to integrate the unique understandings and skills that other professions have produced regarding conflict and resolution?
- How can we use this knowledge to improve the ways we impact mediator learning so as to better achieve these goals?
- Locating potential synergies between psychology and conflict resolution will allow us to take a few small steps toward answering these questions. And small steps, as we learn in mediation, are precisely what are needed to achieve meaningful results. Why should we consider the possibilities of ego defenses or solution-focused mediation? For the same reasons we consider the potential utility of a variety of interventions – because they allow us to understand conflict and enter it in unique and useful ways.
- The logical chain that connects conflict resolution with psychology is simple yet inexorable and logically rigorous, which proceeds as follows:
- It is possible for people to disagree with each other without experiencing conflict.
- What distinguishes conflict from disagreement is the presence of what are commonly referred to as "negative" emotions, such as anger, fear, guilt, and shame.
- Thus, *every* conflict, by definition, contains an indispensible emotional element.
- Conflicts can only be reached and resolved in their emotional location by people who have acquired emotional processing skills, or what Daniel Goleman broadly describes as "emotional intelligence."
- The discipline that is most familiar with these emotional dynamics is psychology.
- Therefore, mediation can learn from psychology how to be more effective in resolving conflicts.

This logic alone should be sufficient to prompt a deeper assessment of psychological research and technique. Yet, considering the problem from a deeper perspective, we all know that no clear line can be drawn in life that allows us to separate our emotions from our ideas, or neurophysiology from behavior. Quite simply, we are all emotional beings and must discover their inner logic if we do not want to be trapped by them.

Deeper still, when we distinguish, simplify, or isolate different aspects of a problem, we disregard their essential unity, and with it, countless opportunities to resolve critically important conflicts and disagreements, simply by approaching them with a pre-determined, single-minded, *particular* point of view, no matter how profound or useful it may happen to be.

There is an equally simple, inexorable, and logically rigorous analysis based on a few simple philosophical assumptions that point us in a different direction. It goes like this: No two human beings are the same. No single human being is the same from one moment to the next. The interactions and relationships between human beings are complex, multi-determined, subtle, and unpredictable. Conflicts are even more complex, multi-determined, subtle, and unpredictable. Most conflicts take place beneath the surface, well below the superficial topics over which people are fighting and frequently hidden from their conscious awareness. [For more, see my book, *The Crossroads of Conflict: A Journey into the Heart of Dispute Resolution,* Janis Publications 2006.]

Thus, each person's attitudes, intentions, intuitions, awareness, context, and capacity for empathetic and honest emotional communication has a significant impact on their experience of conflict and capacity for resolution. As a result, *no one* can know objectively or in advance how to resolve anyparticular conflict, as anything chaotic and rapidly changing cannot be successfully predicted or managed.

For this reason, it is impossible to teach anyone how to resolve a conflict. Instead, we need to develop their skills, improve their awareness and self-confidence, and help them develop a broad range of diverse ideas and techniques that may or may not succeed depending on inherently unpredictable conditions. Moreover, we have known since John Dewey that learning is accelerated when it is connected to doing. Yet we continue to train mediators based on a set of false assumptions.

As an illustration of why it is important to take a different approach to mediator learning, consider these questions, directed primarily to those who are already experienced mediators:

- What have you learned since you began mediating that you wish had been included in your training?
- What are the training values that seem to you to flow naturally from the mediation process?
- Were these values reflected in the way your training was actually conducted? If not, how might they have been?
- How did you learn the *art* of mediation – and especially, how did you learn to be more intuitive, empathetic, openhearted, and wise?
- What skills would you like to be able to develop in the future, and how might these be incorporated in the way mediation training is conducted?

Every mediator to whom I have asked these questions has easily identified a number of important topics that were not covered in their training, but were critical lessons that they discovered only after they started mediating. Here are some of the responses mediators in a recent training I conducted gave regarding what they wished they had been taught:

- Ways of using *brief therapy* and similar psychologically based techniques in mediation;
- Detailed techniques for responding *uniquely* to each negative emotion; i.e., fear, anger, shame, jealousy, pain and grief;
- Coaching skills for working with individual parties in caucus
- Methods for increasing emotional intelligence;
- Ways of discovering what people think or want subconsciously, and of bringing them into conscious awareness;
- Facilitation and public dialogue skills for working with groups;
- Consulting skills for working with organizations on systems design;
- Better ways of analyzing the narrative structure of conflict stories and a list of techniques for transforming them;
- Better techniques for option generating and "expanding the pie";
- Learning when to take risks and mediate "dangerously";
- Ways of becoming more aware of and responding to the "energies" and "vibrations" of conflict;
- How to develop, calibrate and fine-tune intuition, wisdom, and insight;
- Techniques for surfacing, clarifying, and encouraging people to act based on shared values;
- Ways of gaining permission to work with people on a spiritual or heartfelt level;
- Methods for opening heart-to-heart conversations;
- Knowing how to strike the right balance between head and heart;
- Improved techniques for responding to negativity and resistance;
- How to maintain the right balance between control and chaos;
- Helping people reach deeper levels of resolution, including forgiveness and reconciliation;
- Ways of addressing the underlying systemic issues and chronic sources of conflict;
- How to transition into positive action, prevention, and systems design in organizational conflicts;
- Techniques for maintaining balance and equanimity and avoiding frustration and self-doubt when conflicts don't settle;
- Ways of addressing our own unresolved conflicts and making sure our emotions and judgments don't get in our way.

Many of these directly concern the subject matter of this book, and the interplay between psychology and conflict resolution. But what is equally interesting about these responses is that the way we *teach* mediation often does not conform to the core values and principles we *practice* in the mediation process, or to what we know is successful in reaching people who are in conflict, or to what stimulates our learning, or even to how we would most like to be taught.

As I have described elsewhere, values are essentially priorities and integrity-based choices. They can be found both in what we do and what we do not do, in what we grow accustomed to and what we are willing to tolerate. They are openly and publicly expressed, acted on repeatedly, and upheld when they run counter to self-interest. In this way, they are *creators* of integrity and responsibility, builders of optimism and self-esteem, and definitions of who we are. They become manifest and alive through action, including the action of sincere declaration.

At a deeper level, we all communicate values by what we do and say, by how we behave, and by who we become when we are in conflict. While these values are often inchoate and difficult to articulate, beneath many commonly recognized mediation practices we can identify a set of values, even *meta-values* that, in my view, represent our best practices as a profession. Our most fundamentalvalues appear and become manifest to others when we:

- Show up and are present: physically, mentally, emotionally, and spiritually;
- Listen empathetically to what lies hidden beneath words;
- Tell the truth without blaming or judgment;
- Are open-minded, open-hearted, and unattached to outcomes;
- Search for positive, practical, satisfying outcomes;
- Act collaboratively in relationships;
- Display *unconditional* authenticity, integrity, and respect;
- Draw on our deepest intuition;
- Are on both parties' sides at the same time;
- Encourage diverse, honest, heartfelt communications;
- Always act in accordance with our core values and principles;
- Are ready for anything at every moment;
- Seek completion and closure;
- Are able to let go, yet abandon no one.

While not everyone will accept these values, merely articulating, debating, and engaging in dialogue over them, considering how to implement them, and deciding to commit and live by them, will automatically give rise to a higher order of values – the value of *having* values. Practicing them over time – not solely in what we say or do, but how we say and do it, will initiate to the highest order of values – the value of *being* what we value.

By living our values, we become what we practice, integrating who we are with what we preach and do. This is the deeper message of mediation: That by continually and collaboratively searching for positive solutions to conflict, bringing them into conscious attention, living them as fully as possible, and developing the theories, practices, processes, and relationships that allow others do the same, we enhance our relationship to the mediation process as a whole and build a collaborative community of reflective, emotionally intelligent practitioners.

Thus, to be fully realized, our values have to be reflected not merely in our practice, but in all aspects of our personal lives, including the ways we ourselves handle conflict, teach mediation, and interact with those who wish to learn it. Yet many mediators' lives are filled with intense adversarial conflicts, many mediation trainings are conducted in ways that do not conform to its core values, and many mediators interact with students in ways that undermine their ability tolearn.

For example, when trainers do not acknowledge or respect differences between cultures, styles, and diverse approaches to conflict; when they try to promote one-size-fits-all models as applicable to all circumstances; when they downplay and ignore the role of emotions,or heartfelt communications; when they do not pay attention to the diverse ways people learn, or even to the ways people are seated in the classroom; when they ignore the systemic sources of conflict; or when they fail to listen and learn from those they are teaching, we can say that the processes they are using are not congruent with the values they espouse. Here is a simple, concrete illustration.

Howard Gardner at Harvard University has famously described the diverse ways people learn using the idea of *multiple intelligences.* The core of his theory is a recognition that people think and learn differently. Gardner believes there is not "one form of cognition that cuts across all human thinking, "but that traditional notions of intelligence are misleading because I.Q. tests focus primarily or exclusively only on two areas of competence: logic and linguistics." Instead, Gardner believes there are eight areas of intelligence that account for the range of human potential:

1. *Linguistic Intelligence,* or the capacity to use the written or spoken language to express ourselves
2. *Logical-Mathematical Intelligence,* or the ability to understand scientific principles or logic systems;
3. *Spatial Intelligence,* or the ability to conceptualize spatial relationships
4. *Bodily Kinesthetic Intelligence,* or the ability to use our whole body or parts of it to solve problems, make things, or express ideas and emotions through movement
5. *Musical Intelligence,*or the ability to "think" in music, be able to recognize patterns, and manipulate them
6. *Interpersonal Intelligence,* or the ability to understand other people and form and build strong, productive relationships
7. *Intrapersonal Intelligence,* or the ability to understand ourselves and know who we are, including our strengths and limitations
8. *Naturalist Intelligence,*or the ability to see and understand the interrelationship and interdependence of all living things and have a special sensitivity to the physical features of the natural world

While each of us may have quibbles with this list and perhaps wish to suggest alternative forms of intelligence, such as emotional, heart or spiritual, and political intelligence, it is clear that most mediations and conflict resolution training programs narrowly focus on linguistic and logical skills and ignore other forms of intelligence, intervention styles, and conflict processing skills that might contribute significantly to success in mediation.

Even the word *training* is problematic. There are, for example, fundamental differences betweenvarious approaches to teaching and learning, and these same differences can be found in the ways we seek to resolve conflicts. We can distinguish, for example:

- *Lecture and Recitation,* which involve rote memorization and recall of facts, and result in a transfer of information, yet often end in testing and forgetting
- *Education and Courses,* which involve exposure to ideas, specialized theories and practical techniques that result in learning and understanding, yet often end in disputation and Talmudic clashes of opinion over minutia
- *Training and Workshops,* which involve group discussion and result in improved technical skills, competency and confidence, yet often end in mechanical repetition, inflexibility, and inability to handle problems not addressed in the training
- *Practice and Exercises,* which involve role plays and practical drills, and result in increased self-confidence and some degree of flexibility, yet often end in improving skills without also improving the understanding needed to successfully implement them
- *Personal Development and Seminars,* which involve discovery, self-awareness, and self-actualization, and result in authenticity, integrity and personal transformation, yet often end in nonengagement with others
- *Meditation and Retreats,* which involve insight and concentration, and result in wisdom, spiritual growth, and transcendence, yet often end in nothing ever changing or being accomplished, and a lack of interest in improving others

These diverse forms of learning invisibly shift our focus, activity, and forms of interaction from an orientation toward memorizing, to one of knowing, to one of understanding, to one of doing, to one of being. As we transition to deeper levels of capability in our practice, understanding, and commitment to conflict resolution, we require learning methods that allow us to develop more collaborative, democratic, self-aware, and diversely competent skills as mediators.

While every learning process has a value and each has times and circumstances that justify and make it successful, in my experience, those that improve our ability to work through the *emotional,*psychological, and heart-based underpinnings of conflict – especially our own – create the greatest leverage in terms of the development of values, integrity, and overall capacity building.

Approaching the problem of mediation competency, learning, and training design from this point of view suggests a number of interesting questions we can begin asking prospective mediators, to improve their psychological awareness, develop their emotional intelligence, and facilitate the design of more advanced training programs. For example:

- What are the most significant transformational learning experiences you have had?
- What made them significant or transformational for you?
- What did these experiences have in common that you might want to incorporate into a training experience?
- *Why* attend this training? What do you really want to achieve?
- What are your larger goals and priorities, and how might this training support them?
- What could block your ability to achieve these goals and priorities, and how could these obstacles be anticipated and overcome?
- What specifically do you want to be taught? How did you learn *that*?
- What do you think will be the best way of teaching what you want to learn?
- Who else should be trained? Why them? Who should not be trained? Why not?
- Who would be the ideal trainer? Why? Who would not? Why?
- What values, ideas, and skills do you most want to learn?
- How might those values, ideas, and skills be built into the content and process of the training?
- How will the training actually result in changed behavior? How should you be supported in changing?
- How might others support you in changing?
- Will the training lead to improved systems, processes and relationships? If so, how?
- How will you learn the *art* of what you want to do?
- Should the training encourage you to participate, think critically, and feel free to be yourself? How?
- How might your future needs and problems be anticipated in the content and process of the training?
- How will you know whether the training has been effective?
- Based on the answers to these questions, how should the training be designed and conducted?

The answers to these questions may collaterally help stimulate a number of potential growth areas in the field of conflict resolution, such as marital mediation between couples who would like to improve their relationship using mediation skills; applying conflict resolution systems design skills to a broad range of social, economic, and political issues; mediating the connections between families, community groups, workplaces, organizations; integrating conflict resolution skills into teambuilding and project management workshops; extending school mediations to encourage parents and teachers to work through their personal conflicts along with the children; working with a broad range of hospital and health care disputes that flow from the need to process grief, guilt, rage, and loss; and new ideas for resolving intractable international conflicts.

Part of the object of a truly *meditative* approach to education ought to be to encourage students to become responsible for their own learning, and teachers to be responsible for finding the deepest, most profound and effective way of supporting them. One way of doing so, inspired by paradoxical approaches to therapy, is by asking students to complete the following questionnaire *before* their training, then discuss their answers

Pre-Training Evaluation

Please rate your expectations regarding the session we are about to have, and how you expect to participate on a scale of 1 to 10, 10 being highest.
1. *How valuable an experience do you plan to have?* (1 = terrible, 10 = fantastic):
2. *How participative and engaged do you plan to be?* (1 = asleep, 10 = extremely excited):
3. *How much risk do you plan to take?* (1 = none, 10 = serious adventure):
4. *How open, honest and constructive do you plan to be?* (1 = silent, 10 = painfully honest):
5. *How willing are you to listen nondefensively and nonjudgmentally to others?* (1 = doing email, 10 = completely open):
6. *How responsible do you feel for your own learning?* (1 = not at all, 10 = entirely):
7. *How responsible do you feel for the learning of others?* (1 = not at all, 10 = totally):
8. *How committed are you to implementing what you learn?* (1 = amnesia, 10 = complete commitment):
[Based in part on work by Peter Block]

Applying these ideas to conflict resolution, we all know intuitively that mediators are not immune from conflicts, and that we will become better dispute resolvers by working through and resolving our own conflicts. It therefore makes sense for us to incorporate into the mediation training process the psychological components that will allow people to work directly on resolving their personal conflicts. At present, few mediation programs allow or encouragethem to do so.

In the end, we *are* the technique. As imperfect as we are, it is who we *are* that forms the path to resolution, and that same path invites us to become better human beings, simply in order to become better mediators. This realization returns mediation to its *human* origins and essence, as an exercise not solely in empathy and compassion, but in creative problem solving, emotional clarity, heartfelt wisdom, and social collaboration.

It is my hope that this book by Fredrike Bannink will begin to change our ideas about the usefulness of psychological approaches in mediation. Hopefully, these ideas, exercises, and practices will encourage us to look more deeply and wisely at the world within, as well as the world without, and assist us in finding ways to translate our own suffering into methods and understandings that will lead to a better, less hostile and adversarial world.

References

Aristotle. (2004). *The Nicomachean ethics* (J. A. K. Thomson, Trans.). London: Penguin Classics.

Arts, W., Hoogduin, C. A. L., Keijsers, G. P. J., Severeijnen, R., & Schaap, C. (1994). A quasi-experimental study into the effect of enhancing the quality of the patient-therapist relationship in the outpatient treatment of obsessive-compulsive neurosis. In S. Brogo & L. Sibilia (Eds.), *The patient–therapist relationship: Its many dimensions*. Rome: Consiglio Nazionale delle Ricerche.

Bakker, J. M., & Bannink, F. P. (2008). Oplossingsgerichte therapie in de psychiatrische praktijk [Solution focused therapy in psychiatric practice]. *Tijdschrift voor Psychiatrie, 1*, 55–59.

Bannink, F. P. (2005). De kracht van oplossingsgerichte therapie: een vorm van gedragstherapie [The power of solution-focused therapy: A form of behavior therapy]. *Gedragstherapie, 38*(1), 5–16.

Bannink, F. P. (2006a). *Oplossingsgerichte mediation [Solution-focused mediation]*. Amsterdam: Pearson.

Bannink, F. P. (2006b). Oplossingsgerichte mediaton [Solution-focused mediation]. *Tijdschrift Conflicthantering, 6*, 143–145.

Bannink, F. P. (2006c). *Oplossingsgerichte vragen. Handboek oplossingsgerichte gespreksvoering [Solution-focused questions. Handbook of solution-focused interviewing]*. Amsterdam: Pearson.

Bannink, F. P. (2006d). De geboorte van oplossingsgerichte cognitieve gedragstherapie [The birth of solution-focused cognitive behavior therapy]. *Gedragstherapie, 39*(3),171–183.

Bannink, F. P. (2007a). *Gelukkig zijn en geluk hebben. Zelf oplossingsgericht werken [Being happy and being lucky. Solution focused self-help]*. Amsterdam: Pearson.

Bannink, F. P. (2007b). Solution focused brief therapy. *Journal of Contemporary Psychotherapy, 37*(2), 87–94.

Bannink, F. P. (2007c). Oplossingsgerichte therapie [Solution focused brief therapy]. *Maandblad Geestelijke volksgezondheid MGv, 10*, 836–848.

Bannink, F. P. (2008a). Solution focused mediation. The future with a difference. *Conflict Resolution Quarterly, 25*(2), 163–183.

Bannink, F. P. (2008b). Vergelding of verzoening [Retaliation or reconciliation]. *Forum voor Conflictmanagement, 1*, 26–28.

Bannink, F. P. (2008c). Solution focused mediation. Retrieved from http://www.mediate.com//articles/banninkF1.cfm

Bannink, F. P. (2008d). Posttraumatic success: Solution focused brief therapy. *Brief Treatment and Crisis Intervention, 7*, 1–11.

Bannink, F.P. (2008e). Solution focused mediation. *The Jury Expert, 20*(3), 13–23. Retrieved from http://www.astcweb.org/public/publication/issue.cfm/September/2008/20/3/19

Bannink, F. P. (2008f). Visitor, complainant, customer. Motivating clients to change in mediation. Retrieved from http://www.mediate.com//articles/banninkF2.cfm

Bannink, F. P. (2009a). Supermediators. Retrieved from http://www.mediate.com//articles/banninkF3.cfm

Bannink, F.P. (2009b). Columns *conflict inzicht [Column conflict insight]*. Utrecht: Stili Novi.

Bannink, F. P. (2009c). Building positive emotions in mediation. Retrieved from http://www.mediate.com//articles/banninkF4.cfm.

Bannink, F. P. (2009d). Solution focused conflict management in teams and in organisations. *InterAction, The Journal of Solution Focus in Organisations, 1*(2), 11–25.

Bannink, F. P. (2010a). *1001 Solution Focused Questions.* New York: Norton (in press).

Bannink, F. P. (2010b). Successful scaling in mediation. Retrieved from http://www.mediate.com//articles/banninkF5.cfm

Baruch Bush, R. A., & Folger, J. P. (2005). *The promise of mediation. The transformative approach to conflict.* San Francisco: Jossey-Bass.

Bateson, G. (1972). *Steps to an ecology of mind.* Chicago: The University of Chicago Press.

Baumgartner, T., Heinrichs, M., Vonleuthen, A., Fischbacher, U. & Fehr, E. (2008). Oxytocin shapes the neural circuitry of trust and trust adaptation in humans. *Neuron, 58,* 639–650.

Beckhard, R., & Harris, R. (1987). *Managing organizational transitions* (2nd ed.). Reading, MA: Addison-Wesley.

Berg, I. K., & Szabo, P. (2005). *Brief coaching for lasting solutions.* New York: Norton.

Bergin, A. E., & Garfield, S. L. (Eds.). (1994*). The handbook of psychotherapy and behavior change* (4th ed.). New York: Wiley.

Beutler, L. E., Malik, M. L., Alimohamed, S., Harwood, T. M., Talebi, H., & Noble, S. (2004). Therapist variables. In M. J. Lambert (Ed.), *Bergin and Garfield's handbook of psychotherapy and behavior change.* New York: Wiley.

Bruin, J. H. de (2008). Bemiddeling deur waarheid na versoening: Die slothoofdstuk op die traumatiese nalatenskap van die Suid-Afrikaanse geskiedenis? [Mediation through truth after reconciliation: The final chapter of the traumatic legacy of South African history?] *Forum voor Conflictmanagement, 1,* 17–25.

Bunker, B. B. (2000). Managing conflict through large-group methods. In M. Deutsch & P. T. Coleman (Eds.). *The handbook of conflict resolution.* San Francisco: Jossey-Bass.

Burns, G. W. (2001). *101 healing stories: Using metaphors in therapy.* New York: Wiley.

Cantwell, P., & Holmes, S. (1994). Social construction: A paradigm shift for systemic therapy and training. *The Australian and New Zealand Journal of Family Therapy, 15,* 17–26.

Cauffman, L. (2003). *Oplossingsgericht management & coaching [Solution focused management & coaching].* Utrecht, The Netherlands: Lemma.

Cialdini, R. B. (1984). *Persuasion. The psychology of influence.* New York: Collins.

Clement, P. W. (1994). Quantitative evaluation of 26 years of private practice. *Professional Psychology: Research and Practice, 25*(2), 173–176.

Breslau, K., & Heron, K. (2000). The debriefing: Bill Clinton. Retrieved from http://www.wired.com/wired/archive/8.12/clinton.html

Cloke, K. (2001). *Mediating dangerously: The frontiers of conflict resolution.* San Francisco: Jossey-Bass.

Cloke, K. (2005). Why every conflict breaks your heart: Conflict as a spiritual crisis. *ACResolution, 5*(1), 16–21.

Cloke, K. (2006). *The crossroads of conflict: A journey into the heart of dispute resolution.* Calgary, Canada: Janis.

Cloke, K. (2009). Bringing oxytocin into the room: Notes on the neurophysiology of conflict. Retrieved from http://www.mediate.com//articles/cloke8.cfm

Coleman, P. T. (2000). Some guidelines for developing a creative approach to conflict. In M. Deutsch & P. T. Coleman (Eds.), *The handbook of conflict resolution* (pp. 355–365)*.* San Francisco: Jossey-Bass.

Covey, S. R. (1989). *The seven habits of highly rffective people. Powerful lessions in personal vhange.* New York: Fireside Books, Simon & Schuster.

Csikszentmihalyi, M. (1997). *Finding flow.* New York: Basic Books.

De Bono, E. (1985). *Conflicts: A better way to resolve them.* London: Penguin.

De Jong, P., & Berg, I. K. (1997). *Interviewing for solutions.* Pacific Grove, CA: Brooks/ Cole.

De Shazer, S. (1984). The death of resistance. *Family Process, 23,* 79–93.

De Shazer, S. (1985). *Keys to solution in brief therapy.* New York: Norton.

De Shazer, S. (1988). *Clues: Investigation solutions in brief therapy.* New York: Norton.

De Shazer, S. (1991). *Putting difference to work.* New York: Norton.

De Shazer, S. (1994). *Words were originally magic.* New York: Norton.

De Waal, F. B. M. (2000). Primates – A natural heritage of conflict resolution. *Science, 289,* 586–590.

Deutsch, M., & Coleman, P. T. (Eds.). *The handbook of conflict resolution.* San Francisco: Jossey-Bass.

Dolan, Y. (1998). *One small step.* Watsonville, CA: Papier-Mache.

Duncan, B. L., Miller, S. D., & Sparks, A. (2004). *The heroic client: A revolutionary way to improve effectiveness through client-directed, outcome-informed therapy.* San Francisco: Jossey-Bass.

Duncan, B. L. (2005). *What's right with you?* Deerfield Beach, FL: Health Communications.

D'Zurilla, T. J., & Goldfried, M. R. (1971). Problem solving and behavior modification. *Journal of Abnormal Psychology, 78,* 107–126.

Einstein, A. (1954). *Ideas and opinions.* New York: Crown.

Fisher, R., & Ury, W. (1981). *Getting to yes: Negotiating agreement without giving in.* New York: Penguin.

Foa, U. G., & Foa, E. B. (1975). *Resource theory of social exchange.* Morristown, NJ: General Learning Press.

Frankl, V. E. (1963). *Man's search for meaning.* New York: Washington Square Press, Simon & Schuster.

Fredrickson, B. L. (2000). Cultivating positive emotions to optimize health and well-being. *Prevention & Treatment, 3.* Retrieved from http://journals.apa.org/prevention

Fredrickson, B. L. (2003). The value of positive emotions. *American Scientist, 91,* 330–335.

Fredrickson, B. L. (2009). *Positivity.* New York: Crown.

Furman, B., & Ahola, T. (2007). *Change through cooperation. Handbook of reteaming.* Helsinki, Sweden: Helsinki Brief Therapy Institute.

Gingerich, W. J.,& Eisengart, S. (2000). Solution-focused brief therapy: A review of the outcome research. *Family Process, 39,* 477–498.

Gladwell, M. (2005). *Blink.* London: Penguin.

Glasl, F. (1977). *Konfliktmanagement.* Bern, Germany: Paul Haupt.

Goei, S. L., & Bannink, F. P. (2005). Oplossingsgericht werken in remedial teaching [Solution focused interviewing in remedial teaching]. *Remediaal, Tijdschrift voor leer – en gedragsproblemen in het vo/be, 5*(3), 19–26.

Gordon, K. C., Baucom, D. H., Epstein, N., Burnett, C. K., & Rankin, L. A. (1999). The interaction between marital standards and communication patterns. *Journal of Marital and Family Therapy, 25,* 211–223.

Haynes, J. M., Haynes, G. L., & Fong, L. S. (2004). *Mediation, positive conflict management.* Albany, NY: State University of New York.

Hebb, D. O. (1949). *The organization of behavior: A neuropsychological theory.* New York: Wiley.

Hiatt, D., & Hargrave, G. E. (1995). The characteristics of highly effective therapists in managed behavioral providers networks. *Behavioral Healthcare Tomorrow, 4*, 19–22.

Isebaert, L. (2005). *Kurzzeittherapie – ein praktisches Handbuch.* Stuttgart, Germany: Thieme.

Isen, A. M. (2005). A role for neuropsychology in understanding the facilitating influence of positive affect on social behavior and cognitive processes. In C. R. Snyder & S. J. Lopez, *Handbook of positve psychology* (pp. 528–540). New York: Oxford University Press.

Kazdin, A. E. (2006). Arbitrary metrics: Implications for identifying evidased treatments. *American Psychologist, 61*, 42–49.

Keeva, S. (2004). Apology and the law. *ABA Journal, 90*, n.p.

Kelman, H. C. (2005). Building trust among enemies: The central challenge for international conflict resolution. *International Journal of Intercultural Relations, 29*, 639–650.

Keijsers, G. P. J., Schaap. C. P. D. R., & Hoogduin, C. A. L. (2000). The impact of interpersonal patient and therapist behavior on outcome in cognitive behavior therapy: A review of empirical studies. *Behavior Modification, 24*, 264–297.

Kilmann, R. H., & Thomas, K. W. (1977). Developing a forced-choice measure of conflict-handling behavior: The mode instrument. *Educational and Psychological Measurement, 37*, 309–325.

Lambert, M., Burlingame, G., Umphress, V., Vermeersch, D., Clouse, G., & Yanchar, S. (1996). The reliability and validity of the outcome questionnaire. *Clinical Psychology and Psychotherapy, 3*, 249–258.

Lazare, A. (2004). *On apology.* New York: Oxford University Press.

Lazarus, R. S. (2000). Toward better research on stress and coping. *American Psychologist, 55*, 665–673.

Lewicki, R. J., & Wiethoff, C. (2000). Trust, trust development and trust repair. In M. Deutsch & P. T. Coleman (Eds.), *The handbook of conflict resolution: Theory and practice* (pp. 86–107). San Francisco: Jossey-Bass.

Macdonald, A. (2007). *Solution-focused therapy. Theory, research & practice.* London: Sage.

McCullough, M. E., & Van Oyen Witvliet, C. (2005). The psychology of forgiveness. In C. R. Snyder & S. J. Lopez, *Handbook of positve psychology* (pp. 446–458). New York: Oxford University Press.

Menninger, K. (1959). The academic lecture on hope. *The American Journal of Psychiatry, 109*, 481–491.

Metcalf, L. (1995). *Counseling toward solutions.* San Francisco, CA: Jossey-Bass.

Meyers, D. G. (2000). Hope and happiness. In J. E. Gillham (Ed.), *The science of optimism & hope.* Phialadelphia, PA: Templeton Foundation.

Miller, S. D., Hubble, M. A., & Duncan, B. L. (1996). *The handbook of solution-focused brief therapy: Foundations, applications and research.* San Francisco: Jossey-Bass.

Miller, S. D., Duncan, B., & Hubble, M. A. (1997). *Escape from Babel: Toward a unifying language for psychotherapy practice.* New York: Norton.

Miller, W. R., & Rollnick, S. (2002). *Motivational interviewing. Preparing people for change* (2nd ed.). New York: Guilford.

Mnooking, R. H. (2000). *Beyond winning. Negotiating to create value in deals and disputes.* London: Belknap Press of Harvard University.

Norcross, J. C. (red.) (2002). *Psychotherapy relationships that work; Therapeutic contributions and responsiveness to patients.* Oxford: Oxford University Press.

O'Hanlon, B. (1999). *Do one thing different.* New York: Quill, Harper Collins.

O'Hanlon, B., & Rowan, R. (2003). *Solution oriented therapy for chronic and severe mental illness.* New York: Norton.

Piper W. E., Ogrodniczuk, J. S., Joyce, A. S., McCallum, M., Rosie, J. S., O'Kelly, J. G., et al. (1999). Prediction of dropping out in time-limited interpretive individual psychotherapy. *Psychotherapy*, *36*, 114–122.

Pruitt, D. G., & Kim, S. H. (2004). *Social conflict: Escalation, stalemate, and settlement*. Boston: McGraw-Hill.

Roeden, J. M.,& Bannink, F. P. (2007a). *Handboek oplossingsgericht werken met licht verstandelijk beperkte clienten [Handbook of solution focused interventions with clients with intellectual disabilities]*. Amsterdam: Pearson.

Roeden, J. M.,& Bannink, F. P. (2007b). Hoe organiseer ik een etentje? Oplossingsgerichte gedragstherapie met een verstandelijk beperkte vrouw [How to organise a dinner? Solution focused behavior therapy with a woman with intellectual disabilities]. *Gedragstherapie*, *40*(4), 251–268.

Rosenhan, J. (1973). On being sane in insane places. *Science*, *179*, 250–258.

Rossi, E. L. (Ed.). (1980). *The nature of hypnosis and suggestion by Milton Erickson (collected papers)*. New York: Irvington.

Salacuse, J. W. (1991). *Making global deals. What every executive should know about negotiating abroad*. New York: Times Business Random House.

Salacuse, J. W. (2000). *The wise advisor. What every professional should know about consulting and counseling*. Westport, CT: Praeger.

Scheinecker, M. (2006). SF-Conflict management and conflict consulting in organisations. In G. Lueger & H. Korn (Eds.), *Solution-focused management*. Munchen, Germany: Rainer Hampp Verlag.

Schelling, T. C. (1960). *The strategy of conflict*. Cambridge MA: Harvard University Press.

Selekman, M. D. (1993). *Pathways to change: Brief therapy solutions with difficult adolescents*. New York: Guilford.

Seligman, M. E. (2002). *Authentic happiness*. New York: Free Press.

Sherif, M., Harvey, O. J. Hoyt, B. J. Hood, W. R., & Sherif, C. W. (1961). *Intergroup conflict and cooperation: Tthe robbers cave experiment*. Norman, OK: University of Oklahoma Book Exchange.

Siegel, D. J. (1999). *The developing mind*. New York: Guilford.

Snyder, C. R., Harris, C., Anderson, J. R., Holleran, S. A., Irving, L. M., Sigmon, S. T., et al. (1991). The will and the ways: Development and validation of an individual-differences measure of hope. *Journal of Personality and Social Psychology*, *60*, 570–585.

Snyder, C. R. (1994). *The psychology of hope*. New York: Free Press.

Snyder, C. R., Lapointe, A. B., Crowson, J. J., & Early, S. (1998). Preferencs of high- and low-hope people for self-referential feedback. *Cognition and Emotion*, *12*, 807–823.

Snyder, C. R. (2002). Hope theory: Rainbows in the mind. *Psychological Inquiry*, *13*, 249–275.

Stam, P., & Bannink, F. P. (2008). De oplossingsgerichte organisatie [The solution focused organization]. *Tijdschrift voor Kinder – en Jeugd Psychotherapie*, *35*(2), 62–72.

Stams, G. J., Dekovic, M., Buist, K, & Vries, L. de (2006). Effectiviteit van oplossingsgerichte korte therapie: Een meta-analyse [Efficacy of solution-focused brief therapy: A meta-analysis]. *Gedragstherapie*, *39*(2) 81–94.

Susskind, L., & Cruikshank, J. L. (1987). *Breaking the impasse: Consensual approaches to resolving public disputes*. New York: Basic Books.

Szmamia, S. J. (2006). Mediator's communication in victim offender mediation/dialogue involving crimes of severe violence: An analysis of opening statements. *Conflict Resolution Quarterly*, *24*(1), 111–127.

Tomori, C., & Bavelas, J. B. (2007). Using microanalysis of communication to compare solution-focused and client-centered therapies. *Journal of Family Psychotherapy*, 18(3), 25–43.

Tompkins, P., & Lawley, J. (2003). *Metaphors in mind.* London: The Developing Company.

Umbreit, M. S. (2001). *The handbook of victim offender mediation: An essential guide to practice and research.* San Francisco: Jossey-Bass.

Von Neumann, J., & Morgenstern, O. (1944). *Theory of games and economic behavior.* Princeton, NJ: Princeton University Press.

Walker, L., Sakai, T., & Brady. K. (2006). Restorative circles: A solution-focused reentry planning process for inmates. *Federal Probation Journal*, 70(1), 1–17.

Walker, L., & Hayashi, L. (2007). Pono Kaulike: A Hawaii criminal court provides restorative justice practices for healing relationships. *Federal Probation Journal*, 71(3), 18–24.

Walter. J. L., & Peller, J. E. (1992). *Becoming solution-focused in brief therapy.* New York: Brunner/Mazel.

Walter, J. L. & Peller, J. E. (2000). *Recreating brief therapy, preferences and possibilities.* New York: Norton.

Wampold, B. E. (2001). *The great psychotherapy debate: Model, methods, and findings.* New York: Erlbaum.

Wampold, B. E., & Bhati, K. S. (2004). Attending to the omissions. A historical examination of evidence-based practice movements. *Professional Psychology: Research and Practice*, 35(6), 563–570.

Watzlawick, P., Weakland, J. H., & Fisch, R. (1974). *Change: Principles of problem formation and problem resolution.* New York: Norton.

Watzlawick, P. (1976). *How real is real? Confucsion, disinformation, communication.* New York: Vintage.

Westra, J. & Bannink, F. P. (2006a). 'Simpele' oplossingen! Oplossingsgericht werken bij mensen met een licht verstandelijke beperking, deel 1 ['Simple' solutions! Solution-focused work with clients with mild intellectual disabilities]. *PsychoPraxis*, 8(4) 158–162

Westra, J. & Bannink, F. P. (2006b). 'Simpele' oplossingen! Oplossingsgericht werken bij mensen met een licht verstandelijke beperking, deel 2 ['Simple' solutions! Solution focused work with clients with mild intellectual disabilities]. *PsychoPraxis*, 8(5) 213–218.

White, M., & Epston, D. (1990). *Narrative means to therapeutic ends.* New York: Norton.

Winslade, J., & Monk, G. (2000). *Narrative mediation. A new approach to conflict resolution.* San Francisco: Jossey-Bass.

Wittgenstein, L. (1968). *Philosophical investigations* (G. E. M. Anscombe, Trans., 3rd ed.). New York: Macmillan.

Wright, R. (2000). *Nonzero. History, evolution & human cooperation.* London: Abacus.

Youssef, C. M., & Luthans, F. (2007). Positive organizational behavior in the workplace: The impact of hope, optimism, and resilience. *Journal of Management*, 33, 774–800.

Zehr, H. (2002). *The little book of restorative justice.* Intercourse, PA: Good Books.

Zehr, H. (2004). Commentary: Restorative justice: Beyond victim–offender mediation. *Conflict Resolution Quarterly*, 22(1–2), 305–315.

Websites

www.abanet.org/dispute
American Bar Association, Section of Dispute Resolution

www.acrnet.org
ACR: Association for Conflict Resolution

www.adrresources.com
Spanish international mediation site

www.astcweb.org
ASTC: American Society of Trial Consultants. Journal: The Jury Expert

www.authentichappiness.com
Seligman, founder of positive psychology

www.brieftherapy.org
O'Hanlon, author solution focused brief therapy

www.brief-therapy.org
Brief Family Therapy Center, Milwaukee: Founders solution-focused brief therapy

www.brieftherapy.org.uk
BRIEF London, England

www.crinfo.org
CRIS: Conflict Resolution Information Service: Narrative mediation

www.ebta.nu
European Brief Therapy Association

www.edwdebono.com
Edward de Bono, author of books on management and conflict resolution

www.fredrikebannink.com
Author of this book

www.gingerich.net
Gingerich: Research on solution focused brief therapy

www.iacm-conflict.org
IACM: International Association for Conflict Management

www.johnwheeler.co.uk
Wheeler, solution focused training, consultation and supervision

www.kennethcloke.com
Mediator and author, writer of the Foreword and Epilogue of this book

www.kevinhogan.com
Hogan, author on influence and persuasion

www.law.harvard.edu
Harvard Law School

www.mediate.com
Mediation Information and Resource Centre

www.mediate.com/world
WFM: World Mediation Forum

www.mediatorswithoutborders.org
Mediators Beyond Borders (MBB)

www.pon.harvard.edu
PON: Program on Negotiation at Harvard Law School

www.reteaming.com
Furman, solution focused teamcoaching

www.solutionsdoc.co.uk
Macdonald: research solution focused brief therapy

www.solworld.org
Sharing and Building Solution Focused Practice in Organisations

www.centerforclinicalexcellence.com
ISTC: Institute for the Study for Therapeutic Change and Partners for Change, Miller

www.transformativemediation.org
Institute for the Study of Conflict Transformation

www.ted.com
Technology, Entertainment, Design (TED). Seligman on Positive Psychology

www.voma.org
VOMA: Victim Offender Mediation Association

Appendices

Protocol: First Meeting

- Building rapport
- What are your best hopes? What else?
- What difference would that make? What else?
- What is already working in the right direction? What else?
  Exceptions, scaling progress
- What would be the next step/ next sign of progress? What else?
- End of meeting feedback

Protocol: Subsequent Meetings

- What is better?
- EARS
- Eliciting: What is happening that is better?
- Amplifying: Details about how does that happen? What do you do to make that happen?
- Reinforcing: Compliments
- Start again: What else is better?
- Scaling progress
- End of meeting feedback

Interactional Matrix

Reporting position	Goal	Hypothetical solution/ Mircale question	Exception
Self	What is your goal in coming here?	What will you be doing differently? What will the other person be doing differently?	What are you doing differently? What is the other person doing differently?
Other	What would the other person say is your goal in coming here?	What would the other person say you will be doing differently?	What would the other person say you are doing differently?
	What would the other person say is his goal in coming here?	What would the other person say he will be doing differently?	What would the other person say he is doing differently?
Detached	What would I say or what would the fly on the wall say is your goal in coming here?	What will I or the fly on the wall see you doing differently?	What would I or the fly on the wall see you doing differently?

A. When this conflict will be resolved, what will you notice that is different about the other person? What else?
B. When this conflict will be resolved, what will the other person notice that is different about you? What else?
C. When this conflict will be resolved and you are being watched by an outside observer, what would this observer notice that is different about your relationship to the other person? What else?

Externalization of the Conflict

Name of the conflict: _____

Conflict has control over me/us   I/we have control over conflict

   0   1   2   3   4   5   6   7   8   9   10

1. Where on the scale of control are you today?
2. Where were you the last time? How did you manage to make progress?
3. If you have the same mark on the scale today, how did you manage to stabilize the situation?
4. If you have a lower mark on the scale today, please indicate what you have done before to reach a higher mark again
5. What did important others in your life notice about you last week? How did that influence their behavior towards you?

Session Rating Scale (SRS V.3.0)

Name _____ Age (Yrs): _____

ID# _____ Sex: M / F

Session # _____ Date: _____

Please rate today's session by placing a mark on the line nearest to the description that best fits your experience.

Relationship

├─────────────────────────────────────┤

Goals and Topics

├─────────────────────────────────────┤

Approach or Method

├─────────────────────────────────────┤

Overall

├─────────────────────────────────────┤

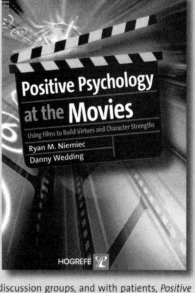
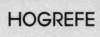

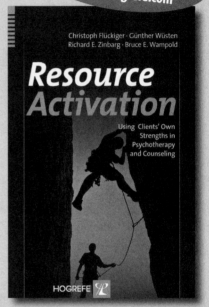